Collecting Antique Toys

Collecting
Antique
Toys

A PRACTICAL GUIDE

by Joseph Doucette
and C. L. Collins

Macmillan Publishing Co., Inc. *New York*
Collier Macmillan Publishers *London*

Macmillan Publishing Co., Inc.
866 Third Avenue, New York, N.Y. 10022
Collier Macmillan Canada, Ltd.

Library of Congress Cataloging in Publication Data

Doucette, Joseph.
Collecting antique toys.
Bibliography: p.
Includes index.
1. Toys—Collectors and collecting. I. Collins,
C. L. II. Title.
NK9509.D6   688.7'2'0750973   81-12340
ISBN 0-02-533010-1   AACR2

10 9 8 7 6 5 4 3 2 1

Printed in the United States of America

To
our fathers,
who would have immensely enjoyed
reading this text

Contents _____

ACKNOWLEDGMENTS

The authors gratefully wish to thank the following people whose contributions and unwavering support aided enormously to the planning, design, and completion of this work: Al Caron; Richard Merrill; Arlene Collins; James Geratowski; Charles Taylor; and Stanley Block and the members of the Marble Collectors Society of America.

Preface

THE AUCTIONEER'S GAVEL crashed to the table, and a resounding "sold" echoed through the hall. Having waited patiently for well over an hour for the advertised Sandwich glass to be brought to the block, we were growing a bit impatient, as well as sore from the hard seats, as each minute seemed to drag into an hour. Two exquisite, signed Handel lamps were sold in quick succession, as were two or three Hummel figurines. Then there was quiet. The mood of the crowd had been steadily declining in enthusiasm for over twenty minutes. Several front-row seats had been vacated and had stayed empty as many members of the gallery filtered out of the hall.

The auctioneer was aware of the crowd's impatience and seemed to know how to handle the problem. He took a moment and announced that our long-awaited glassware would be sold immediately following an assorted lot of old cast-iron and tin toys. No sooner had this statement been issued than the entire mood of the auction seemed to change. A number of people began to drift toward the front of the hall and filled the seats that had been vacated. More than just a few of the folks seated around us suddenly sat erect and directed their full attention toward the podium. The atmosphere was charged with an excitement that we had not witnessed earlier. Even the background chatter stopped, as though in anticipation of an upcoming event of some importance. Then came the toys.

The first toy to be brought up was a cast-iron bank in the shape of an old Ford taxi. It was orange in color and had a driver, and its final selling price was more than enough to arouse our attention. An old paper-covered locomotive and a number of small iron trucks were next to be auctioned. The final bid on each piece was, again, simply astounding.

The last toy to be sold was a very early steam-operated train with two tin boxcars. The auctioneer explained that the toy was designed to be operated by filling the body (boiler) of the locomotive with water and then sliding a small alcohol burner underneath it. When the water reached its boiling point, steam would push out of the openings and force the pistons forward. This action, in turn, would cause the wheels to move, and the train would go huffing and puffing around the wooden circle of track. It was this toy that caused the most interest, even though the cars were badly chipped. In fact, this train brought the highest price paid for a single piece at the auction. To our further amazement, after the bidding was over and the toy was sold for almost $2,000, many people clapped their hands and cheered the buyer.

Our first exposure to the antique-toy world left us mumbling, "What do people see in these old toys?"

This scenario may sound familiar to you. The 1970s have witnessed a nostalgia and collectibles explosion, and toy collecting especially has skyrocketed. There has been a dramatic increase in the popularity of antique toys, trains, and banks. Collectors avidly seek out these childhood mementos at flea markets, antique shops, yard sales, and auctions. Clubs and other organizations have been formed by toy enthusiasts, and their membership lists increase daily.

Some collectors specialize in and collect only one type of toy; others collect representative samples from the major categories of toys. Regardless of the method of acquisition, millions of Americans find collecting and researching antique toys to be exceptionally rewarding, enjoyable, and challenging, whether they are interested in the history and development of a certain toy, toy type, or company or in the mechanics and aesthetics of these early toys.

This book is designed to be simply a guide to the rapidly growing field of toy collecting. Serving as an introduction to the field of antique toys, this is the book that we would have found useful when we started collecting. It will, we hope, clear up many of the common problems faced by the novice collector.

We wish good luck to all collectors, whether they be novice or advanced, and we hope that our contribution to the field will be of interest and service to all.

Collecting Antique Toys

CHAPTER 1

What Compels People to Collect Old Toys?

Human beings are an interesting lot indeed. With the possible exception of pack rats, we are the only group of animals who collect objects simply for the sheer pleasure of collecting. Bits of string, old newspapers, matchbook covers, doorknobs, clocks, beer cans, toys, and a million other things are herded together and hoarded to create miniature museums and commentaries on the human condition.

What then is this drive that infects most of us and forces us to amass tons of objects that are, quite often, considered worthless in most circles? What is it that causes us to be insanely jealous of the person who owns a piece that we desire for our own collection? Why is the competition so unusually fierce? We leave it to psychologists and psychiatrists to explain these phenomena.

Toy collecting is perhaps an innate longing for those toys we had as children and would like to own again or for those toys we longed for but could not afford. Perhaps toy collecting is simply an escape, an "out" from the pressures of our normal day-to-day routine. Whatever the reason, the outcome is the same. Collecting, no matter what is being collected, is an extremely enjoyable and relaxing pastime.

In all fields of collecting there are compulsive people, those who eat, sleep, dream, and exist totally in their private little worlds. We mention this problem because collecting can be a costly addiction. No matter what one's justification for his or her toy-collecting habit, whether it be historical significance, aesthetic appeal, or monetary value or gain, the collector must always remember that the objects being traded, bought, sold, researched, and longed for are, after all, only playthings.

A tin ferris wheel (ca. 1900) manufactured by a German toy firm started in the mid-1860s by Ernest Plank of Nuremburg. This tin ferris wheel is hand-painted and revolves when the wheel is turned. Note the groove in the operating wheel that indicates that it could have been attached to a steam engine. Not surprisingly, Plank was a large manufacturer of steam engines. RICHARD MERRILL.

Serious collectors, "addicts," and dealers can be easily spotted at an auction. Look for the bidders who have numbers one through five. In order to get these numbers, they had to arrive three hours before the auction was scheduled to begin. Look for the folks who are eyeing only the rarer toys. They probably have all of the others. Look for familiar faces. Chances are that the people who travel many miles to attend five or six auctions in a row are more than just a little interested in the hobby. Look for those standing at the rear of the gallery. In this position bidders have a clear view of the crowd and can usually see who is bidding against them. Your most serious competition will most probably come from here.

"Addicts" sometimes wear T-shirts with a message, such as "I still play with toys." They occasionally travel to a number of different auctions that happen to fall on the same day and often leave absentee bids on those pieces they especially desire. In addition, they usually belong to four or more toy-related organizations and are known to use the following phrases:

> "It's in mint condition. That's the only condition
> I will consider buying."
> "I had to have it, even though I passed one for half
> that amount last year."
> "It's a very nice toy, but I only collect Ives."
> "It's a good investment. Far better than money in the
> bank."
> "I needed it for a comparison piece. My example has
> more red in it."

A person who exhibits any of these behavior patterns is likely to be more than a casual collector pursuing an enjoyable hobby!

TOYS HAVE A MAGIC ALL THEIR OWN

Old toys, more than most other antique collectibles, tend to exude a sort of hypnotic power over their viewers. They have a definite charisma and charm all their own.

An Eagle Milk and Cream wagon (ca. 1920). Ice wagons and milk wagons seem to have been popular subjects for cast-iron toys, but this example, manufactured by the Hubley Company, has to be one of the nicest. White, with red wheels, it was produced in two sizes. The smaller version had no driver. RICHARD MERRILL.

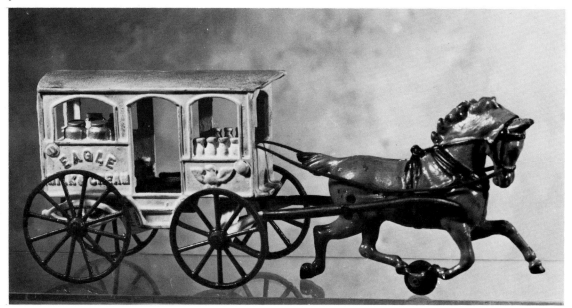

Toys, and play in general, have always had a very important function in society, but until recently this value was overlooked and misunderstood. Through play, roles are developed and expanded upon. Children's personalities develop as a direct outgrowth of their role playing during their formative years. Children are first introduced to the real world through toys and play with other children. As a guide, toys have always been a window through which children first conceptualize the realities of the world. Though many of us are reluctant to admit it as we grow, our toys grow up too, even though their names and shapes and prices change. (It has been said that the only difference between men and boys is the price of their toys!) As we get older,

This page from a 1910 Ives catalog illustrates and describes the complete line of fire brigade toys. Marked "Phoenix," these were some of the finest cast-iron toys ever produced. C. L. COLLINS.

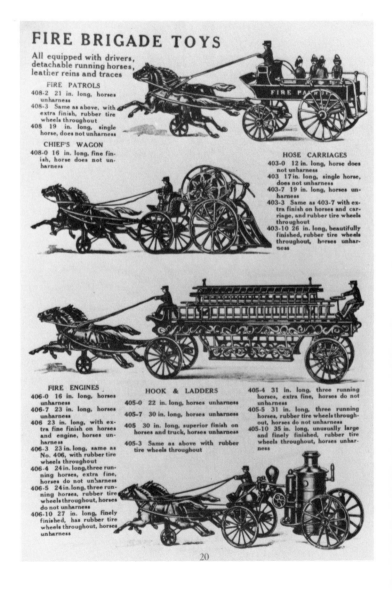

FIRE BRIGADE TOYS

All equipped with drivers, detachable running horses, leather reins and traces

FIRE PATROLS
408-2 21 in. long, horses unharness
408-3 Same as above, with extra finish, rubber tire wheels throughout
408 19 in. long, single horse, does not unharness

CHIEF'S WAGON
408-0 16 in. long, fine finish, horse does not unharness

HOSE CARRIAGES
403-0 12 in. long, horse does not unharness
403 17 in. long, single horse, does not unharness
403-7 19 in. long, horses unharness
403-3 Same as 403-7 with extra finish on horses and carriage, and rubber tire wheels throughout
403-10 26 in. long, beautifully finished, rubber tire wheels throughout, horses unharness

FIRE ENGINES
406-0 16 in. long, horses unharness
406-7 23 in. long, horses unharness
406 23 in. long, with extra fine finish on horses and engine, horses unharness
406-3 23 in. long, same as No. 406, with rubber tire wheels throughout
406-4 24 in. long, three running horses, extra fine, horses do not unharness
406-5 24 in. long, three running horses, rubber tire wheels throughout, horses do not unharness
406-10 27 in. long, finely finished, has rubber tire wheels throughout, horses unharness

HOOK & LADDERS
405-0 22 in. long, horses unharness
405-7 30 in. long, horses unharness
405 30 in. long, superior finish on horses and truck, horses unharness
405-3 Same as above with rubber tire wheels throughout

405-4 31 in. long, three running horses, extra fine, horses do not unharness
405-5 31 in. long, three running horses, rubber tire wheels throughout, horses do not unharness
405-10 35 in. long, unusually large and finely finished, rubber tire wheels throughout, horses unharness

20

bicycles are replaced by motorcycles and recreational vehicles; toy cars, telephones, televisions, stoves, and many other childhood items are pushed aside in favor of functional objects, necessary conveniences, or unnecessary extravagances. However, these items continue to serve the same purpose. The socialization process is developed through role playing. All of the objects around us, all of our possessions, are extensions of this development.

The realization that we all need our toys does not sufficiently explain the behavior of those adults who collect old playthings, actual toys that were once played with by children. These adults purchase toys that were designed for a much younger market. They buy these toys often for enormous sums of money and place them on shelves to display to a few discerning friends. Why? Nostalgia is not the only reason. Neither is competition nor the fellowship that one enjoys with other collectors. There is no single reason but, rather, a combination of many; toy collecting is an enjoyable hobby and one, probably the only one, that allows collectors to reexperience the excitement of their childhoods.

Toys reflect the growth of culture, ideas, inventions, hopes and aspirations, political and moral thought, art and individuality, and the age of the machine. By tracing the development of toys, one can at the same time trace the development of any given society. Inventions and ideas are quite often tested in toys before they are realized in full scale. In much the same way, some scientists write science fiction novels to propose ideas whose time has not yet come. Look around and see which cultures promote war toys, for example, over scientific toys. It is an interesting study in conditioning. As has been stated, toys are an effective escape. By their simplicity of charm and grace they can transport the viewer back to a quieter, less hectic point in time. Holding and examining a fine old toy is often experienced as an aesthetic journey to a bygone era. It is quite ironic to note here that toys have become a type of status symbol. What a surrealistic concept! In fact, many collections have a market value of over $1 million.

TOY COLLECTING IS AN ENJOYABLE HOBBY

Every toy collector has dreamed at least once of an unexpected telephone call from a stranger seeking an appraisal of some toys that were found in the attic. Before the telephone receiver has had a chance to settle back into its cradle, the collector is out of the door and on his way. At the house he is escorted into the living room and shown the toys, which are sitting on a small Victorian table. Resting there are a complete Royal Circus set; an Ives No. 40 engine, tender, and two cars; and a half dozen mechanical banks. The owner says that she knows the toys are valuable and so she is asking $200 for the lot! At this point, the collector is usually awakened by his own heavy breathing.

Impossible? Probably. But the excitement of the search, the dream of the discovery, and the thrill of the find make toy collecting a rewarding hobby.

Everyone can identify with old toys. After all, everyone was a child at one time or another. But it is important to remember that the objects of the toy collector's affection are only playthings that were loved as well as abused by their young owners. Like all hobbies and pastimes, toy collecting should not be taken too seriously. To enjoy the hobby, one should relax, have fun, and not get upset if outbid at an auction.

Some categories of toys are quite expensive. Wise collectors will buy only what they can afford. It is still possible, even though somewhat improbable, that the really rare toy that people are bidding thousands of dollars for can be found en masse in a boarded-up old storeroom. Recently a storeroom full of

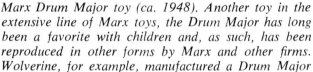

Marx Drum Major toy (ca. 1948). Another toy in the extensive line of Marx toys, the Drum Major has long been a favorite with children and, as such, has been reproduced in other forms by Marx and other firms. Wolverine, for example, manufactured a Drum Major toy in 1937. The differences in these two toys are slight indeed, the major one being the lithography: The toy by Wolverine has only one lithographed shoulder strap instead of two. This Drum Major, a very colorful toy, stands nearly 13½ inches tall. When the toy is wound, the figure bangs away on the drums. Included is a start-and-stop lever. Although a common toy, the Drum Major, like many other Marx toys, is now gaining a following among collectors. RICHARD MERRILL.

toys from the 1930s and 1940s, in brand-new condition, was discovered at the old Louis Marx Company warehouse.

Many people collect toys because they are representative of actual objects in real life, such as trains, cars, and airplanes. The collector who would love to own a full-size, horse-drawn, fire pumper or a real circa 1920 yellow cab is, of course, confronted with a limited supply and probably a lack of storage space. Toys are a bit easier to come by, but even they can create a space problem. It is fun to display pieces, but not to trip over them at every turn. Wise collectors choose items that suit their particular space limitations.

TOY COLLECTING CAN BE PROFITABLE!

As toy collecting has grown in popularity many people have profited greatly by buying and selling toys. As in any other business, there is considerable overhead, especially if you run a shop. Dealers who sell only at shows, and maybe do a mail-order business, probably make out the best. As a business, toy dealing requires considerable expenditures for travel, food, and lodging. The market is so extensive, however, that returns outweigh input by a sizable margin.

To be successful in this business you must be well versed in all types of toys, since you never know what may come your way. This is especially true when you are buying old toys from a new source. Not only must you know whether the toy is an original or a reproduction, but you must also be wary of toys that may have been stolen. You should know, for example, that only three examples of a particular toy are known to exist and that one has recently been stolen. You may find "example number four," but you should be cautious. Many of the advanced collectors and dealers know one another, and when a rare toy is stolen, they know from where it originated. Toy collectors and dealers, by and large, try to protect one another's interests. The bond, in many cases, approaches a fraternal one. This is perhaps one of the nicer aspects of the hobby.

As an investment, toys are probably a good choice. Fine antiques of all types are now being purchased for record prices in anticipation of a good return on the investment. Also, the European market has expanded greatly over the past few years, as shown by the influx of European dealers into the American market. With the rate of exchange in their favor, Europeans are buying as many fine antiques, including toys, as they can get. Before investing a sizable amount of money in toys, you should develop a "feel" for collecting by getting to know the dealers and other collectors, by handling some good old toys, and by attending auctions and visiting museums. We cannot stress this point too strongly.

What toy categories are currently the best investment? That depends on your preferences. Early tin toys of the period from 1870 to 1920 are probably

A Barney Google and Sparkplug comic-strip toy (ca. 1920). One of the most popular comic strips during the 1920s was Barney Google. Barney, his horse Sparkplug, his ostrich Rudi, and a few others peopled the strip until the 1930s, when Snuffy Smith was added. Snuffy eventually took over the strip as Barney's popularity dropped. One of the numerous Barney Google toys produced is the one pictured, with Barney astride his noble steed. Manufactured by the Nifty Company in Germany, this toy is approximately 7½ inches long and is made of lithographed tin. The most common of the Barney Google toys, it works by means of a clockwork mechanism. As Sparkplug walks along, Barney pops up and down and the horse's head and tail move. RICHARD MERRILL.

rising in value at the best rate. Larger pieces are especially desirable. Early American and hand-painted European toys are a very good investment. In addition, the automotive toys (especially the larger cast-iron vehicles) and the comic-strip toys are making an impressive stand. The earlier comic-strip toys are especially strong, but even the later ones, such as Japanese toys from the 1940s and 1950s, are jumping by leaps and bounds. Three or four years ago you could not have given the Japanese toys away, but now they are commanding respectable sums of money. No one really knows why, other than the fact that earlier toys are so difficult to find. One can only venture a guess that a great deal of speculating is occurring. This phenomenon can also be witnessed in the space-toy market. Again, a few years back, you could have found these toys everywhere for only a few dollars. Today, they are sold for $20 to $100 each.

Toy categories that have recently "softened," or are not highly in demand, include the cast-iron, horse-drawn toys. For some reason collecting trends go in cycles, and right now the horse-drawn group is slightly "depressed." The situation may not remain this way for long, however. In fact, by the time this book is published, these types of toys may again be highly sought after.

Another overlooked and modestly priced group is the still banks, with the exception of the very rare examples. Most collectors seek the mechanicals, which are becoming extremely difficult to find. Prior to 1957, many examples of the mechanical-bank group were considered "common." Today, however, even the most seasoned dealer and collector will agree that this term can no longer be applied. The stills are by far more plentiful, and a wise investor should give them serious consideration. In addition, the still banks are enjoyable to collect because they are so diverse in subject matter and construction (see Chapter 4). It has been estimated that prior to 1950 approximately ten thousand different still banks were produced. Materials used in their construc-

From buggy to horseless carriage. Left: *The automobile is a Kenton touring car (ca. 1928–1929). It is approximately 10 inches long and has solid wheels with embossed spokes. There was a variation of this toy produced with actual spoked wheels in addition to a driver and only one passenger.* Right: *This buggy, or Hansom Cab, is 8 inches long and could also be a Kenton product (ca. 1904–1910).* RICHARD MERRILL.

A Speed-Way Coupe (ca. 1930s) is always nice to find in its original box, like the one pictured. The toy itself is in good condition, but the box is somewhat worn and has been repaired with tape. Another toy by the Louis Marx Company, this Speed-Way Coupe measures about 9 inches in length and is lithographed in red with black trim. The tires are white. Included are the original headlight bulbs, which worked by battery power. Luckily, the original battery was not left in this example to rot away the battery compartment. The styling of the auto leads us to believe that the toy was manufactured during the 1930s. RICHARD MERRILL.

tion include tin, pottery, glass, cast iron, composition, wood, pot metal, and plastic.

One of the most interesting and probably most overlooked groups is the safe banks. These banks were constructed to resemble miniature safes and were often equipped with an intricate set of works, which included a combination lock, key, or both. Safe banks can be purchased at a reasonable price and, again, are a good area for investment.

Some toys tend to appreciate in value more quickly than others. As a general "rule of thumb," the rarer or more exotic the toy, the greater the rate of economic growth. Collectors and investors must determine whether they should purchase one hard-to-find and probably more expensive toy or, for the same amount of money, acquire a number of common, lower-priced pieces. This problem can only be resolved by a determination based on the individual's financial situation, outlook on the future, and personal taste. However, we feel that in the near future, with the exception of the unusually fine or rarer pieces, there has to be a leveling off of prices, which should allow some of the more common groups of toys a chance to escalate in value. In addition, as more people enter the toy field, fewer and fewer toys will become available. Thus, a greater demand for those toys still remaining on the market should cause a sharp upswing in the toys' economic potential.

This Maerklin clockwork locomotive was designed for the American market, as shown by the addition of a cowcatcher and a bell to a typically European-styled engine. C. L. COLLINS.

A number of potential growth groups to watch are battery-operated toys, especially banks; tin comic-strip toys from the 1950s and even the 1960s; space toys, robots, and so on; still banks; Marx toys, especially trains; toys with political overtones; and early plastic toys, if there are any left.

It is hoped that no one will collect toys with profit as the sole motivator. The market is highly unstable and prone to considerable fluctuations. You can make money, but doing so takes a great deal of time and knowledge. The competition is fierce between dealers and collectors, and they normally, and we hope will continue to, maintain the highest regard for one another.

CHAPTER 2

Sources of Old Toys

Every collector dreams of finding an attic full of antique toys or trains. Although the likelihood of this happening today is relatively slim, the collector has many options that can possibly make this dream a reality.

CLASSIFIED ADVERTISEMENTS

A classified advertisement in your local newspaper, indicating that you are a collector in search of old toys, can provide many promising leads. Try to answer all of the responses, even though you may be sure doing so will be in vain in many cases. Quite often, even if the person who answered has no collectible toys you want, the simple fact that you were interested enough to respond may prompt him or her to mention you to friends. Word of mouth is your best advertisement.

FRIENDS AND RELATIVES

Another good idea is to purchase most of the toys offered to you, even if you do not need or want them. You may create a future source of supply. In addition, those toys that you do not want can be resold. Once you have established yourself as a serious collector, chances are that some good toys will probably come your way. Let friends and acquaintances know that you are a collector. Quite often, collectors fail to mention this to the people who could probably help them the most. Many times a friend or relative who is unaware of your interests will either throw away or sell an old toy that they consider to have little value.

HISTORICAL SOCIETIES

If there is a local historical society, it may be a good idea to become a member. If anyone would know where old toys are to be found, it would be the members of such an organization. Often a historical society has access to local town archives, which are often excellent sources for potential locations of old toys.

OLD BUILDINGS

If you do have the opportunity to search an old attic, be sure to explore it very carefully. Quite possibly, some old toys were stored in a closet or tucked

An open-air trolley (ca. 1893). During the 1890s, open-air trolleys were a common sight, and so in 1893 the Morton E. Converse Company of Winchendon, Massachusetts, came out with its own version of this popular means of transportation. This is a rather large toy and is made of tin and sheet metal. The body is orange and yellow and the floor is green. The stenciling is in black and was applied by hand. The Lionel Company used Converse bodies on its early 2⅞-inch gauge open trolley.
RICHARD MERRILL.

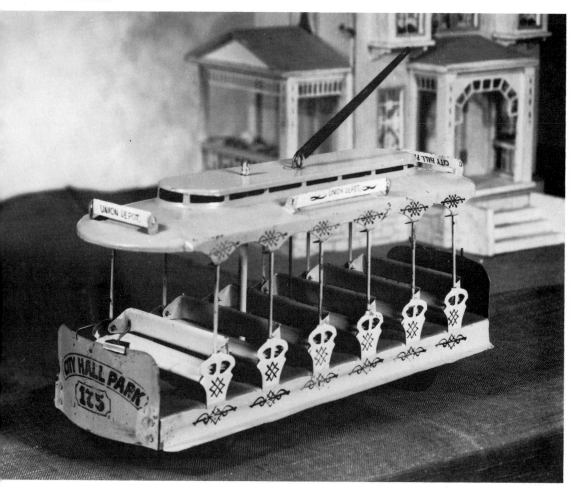

under the eaves or a crawl space. Be sure to check for spaces between the floor and the wall. A small toy may be reposing in any of those places.

There is the story of the toy collector who asked permission to look through an old factory that had at one time manufactured toys. During his search, he discovered a boarded-up doorway that turned out to be an abandoned freight elevator. He obtained permission to pry open the boards and, upon doing so, discovered three or four mechanical banks in their original boxes lying on the elevator floor. Obviously, since they were only toys, they were not considered important enough to remove when the shaft was being boarded up.

Recently, a similar incident took place at the old Marx plant. There is no reason to assume that such events could not happen again.

Remember, millions upon millions of American and imported toys were bought over the past two hundred years, and believing that they all are now in the hands of collectors is unreasonable.

FLEA MARKETS AND YARD SALES

The United States is presently caught up in flea-market and yard-sale fever. Anyone who doubts this has only to read the classified advertisements in

An unusual toy train produced by the Girard Model Works of Girard, Pennsylvania (ca. 1920s). Girard was later bought by the Louis Marx Company. RICHARD MERRILL.

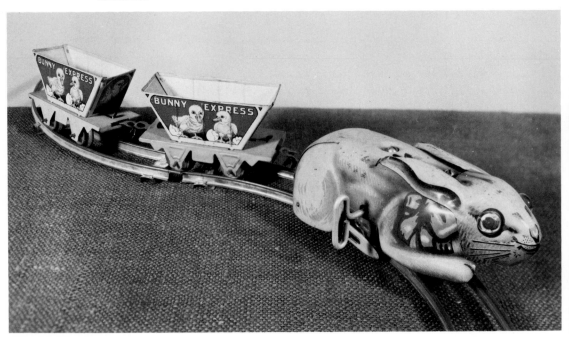

local newspapers. Every weekend the listings get longer, with each market claiming to be better and larger than the others. Ten or fifteen years ago the idea of an outdoor antique market was novel. Today, however, these markets number in the hundreds and are found in all parts of the country.

Many of these markets restrict the wares displayed to only fine antiques. Some promoters have found it profitable to allow dealers to sell a wide variety of merchandise, some of which is plainly "junk." The public has jumped at the opportunity to buy and sell its old furniture, knickknacks, and for that matter, most anything that has been cluttering the house for years.

Yard sales also have become enormously popular for exactly the same reasons. It is true that one can usually sell objects for a bit more at a flea market than at a yard sale. However, a fee must be paid for the privilege of displaying at a flea market. Both are possible sources for old toys.

The key to successful shopping at a flea market is to remember that the advantage almost always rests with the collector. You may have to wade through piles of white elephants in order to find one piece worth buying; but when you do find that piece, the price is usually right. Surprisingly few people are aware that old toys are collectible and command the price often attributed to only "fine" antiques. However, this condition probably will not last too many more years. Generally, when trying to make a purchase, a good idea is to offer a fair price while leaving yourself some margin for profit in case you should later decide to sell the item being acquired.

Flea markets and yard sales are a type of game in which the contestants try to make purchases for as little as possible. If a toy is overpriced, a fair offer is oftentimes enough to pry it loose from its owner. Again, because not everyone is aware of the market, prices quoted are generally far higher or a great deal lower than accepted values. Take a minute to politely explain this fact to a dealer and then make an offer. You may not get the toy, but at least the dealer will appreciate your honesty and goodwill. You can be a successful collector and still play the game fairly.

AUCTIONS

Auctions, like flea markets and yard sales, have proven to be quite an extraordinary phenomenon. Where else can you see relatively sane individuals converge upon the scene to do battle, figuratively speaking, for a highly prized toy? The combatants shake hands, return to their corners, and come out bidding. Occasionally, prices are low. However, prices realized depend entirely on who is or is not present at the auction. If the majority of the bidders are dealers, a collector may stand a good chance of acquiring a piece for a good price. Dealers, in order to realize a profit, will usually not bid a toy beyond what they believe to be its market value. Rather, they will bid to approximately 50 to 75 percent of the price for which they expect to resell the toy. The collec-

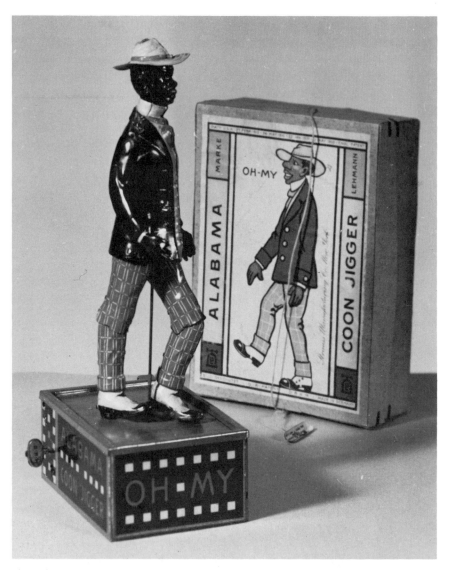

An Alabama Coon Jigger. Manufactured in Germany, this dancing toy was originally called OH-MY. During the 1920s the name was changed to the Alabama Coon Jigger. The toy pictured still has its original box, which adds to its value. This toy was manufactured by the Lehmann Company and came equipped with an on-and-off switch. RICHARD MERRILL.

tor's advantage is in knowing many of the dealers in the local area, so as to be able to correctly assess the competition.

A dealer occasionally will pay an extraordinary high price for a specific toy in order to go on record as having paid a record price. Sometimes this practice is beneficial to the trade; other times it is not. For example, an extremely rare mechanical bank was recently purchased by a dealer at auction for a record price of approximately $18,000. The publicity accorded the auction and the dealer has helped to justify the price paid. In addition, unless the bank has been sold, the dealer owns a type of which only a few examples are known to exist.

On the other hand, another dealer purchased at auction a toy made by the Louis Marx Company during the 1940s for approximately five times its accepted worth. Since this toy was anything but rare, this second dealer received quite a bit of adverse publicity, even in his own circle. Whether or not publicity was the only reason this toy commanded so much money is unclear. What is clear is that this dealer is most certainly going to own the toy for quite some time before he will even be able to make his money back on it.

A Mack dump truck (ca. 1928). One of the most prolific manufacturers of cast-iron automobiles, trucks, and motorcycles was the Arcade Manufacturing Company of Freeport, Illinois. Included in its line was this very fine Mack dump truck. In its original paint and still rigged with the original pulley string (for the dump mechanism), this truck was manufactured along with companion ice and coal trucks which were also Macks. The truck pictured is interesting in that it has spoked wheels and black rubber tires. Another version of the same truck came equipped with solid wheels and white rubber tires. The overall color is gray with gold trim. The length is about 12 inches, and the word Mack is embossed and raised. The driver has a nickel-plated finish and is the same one used on many of the toys from the Arcade line. RICHARD MERRILL.

Competing with other collectors at auction is an entirely different matter. For example, consider a hypothetical situation. At an auction in Connecticut, one of the pieces being offered is a somewhat rare, but not impossible to find, still bank. A collector from New Hampshire has read the ad. After a four-hour drive, our tired but eager collector has arrived at the gallery and located the bank, which happens to be one for which she has been searching for quite some time. The piece is entirely original and in extremely fine condition. The tension mounts as she sits and watches while other bank collectors and dealers enter and examine the bank. After about an hour, the auction begins. Naturally, the bank will not reach the podium until the end of the auction, nearly two hours later. By then the tension is almost unbearable. Finally, the bank is brought up and the bidding starts. Our collector knows that the current market value of "her" bank is only $110, but as the bids reach $75 and $80, this fact tends to be cast aside. She is completely caught up in the heat of the auction as she bids and bids again. The competition is fierce; but finally the bidding is over, the dust is cleared, and the bank is hers, and for *only* $195. "What a bargain," she thinks, as she wraps her prize carefully and places it in her canvas tote bag, the one that she bought specifically for this auction. She pays the cashier and leaves. The fact that she had passed the bank by twice before at a much lower price does not even enter into her consciousness.

This hypothetical situation is not at all farfetched. As is quite often the case at an auction, a collector will bid more for a piece than it is worth just to obtain it for his or her collection. That this price often becomes common knowledge and is quoted in future articles or price guides is unfortunate. The rather inflated price becomes the new market value, when in fact it is the exception rather than the rule. Perhaps the piece is one that a collector needs to finish off a portion of his or her collection, or perhaps the collector was trying to upgrade an example from his or her collection by buying a better example of this bank. These practices are followed by most collectors, especially by those who have most of the items they want. A collector, for any one of many different reasons, may pay more for an article than planned. What is unfortunate is that the reason will probably never be known outside of his or her close circle of friends.

Auction Terms

To the uninitiated, a visit to an auction may seem somewhat like a visit to a foreign country in which a different language is spoken. Following is a discussion of a few of the more familiar terms used at an auction.

No Reserves. When someone consigns a toy to an auction, he or she sometimes has the option to place a minimum acceptable bid on the toy. If the bidding doesn't reach this figure, the piece gets passed or put aside. This is a

A beautiful lithograph of the Baldwin locomotive, Tiger. It is an excellent example of the train-related memorabilia. This lithograph dates from 1878. C. L. COLLINS.

reserve bid. Most auction galleries shy away from this practice because it could reduce their commissions. Before the bidding gets underway, the auctioneer will normally inform the audience that a reserve bid has been placed upon a certain toy.

Premium Charge. A *premium charge* is a practice used by some auction galleries to get a little extra for their efforts. The premium charge is paid for by the buyer. If the premium is 10 percent and the buyer has bid $10, the total cost is $11. With the same premium charge, a $1,000 purchase will cost $1,100. Add a state tax and you have a pretty healthy figure! Keep these added charges in mind when buying toys at an auction.

Commission. Most auction galleries charge the person who consigns a piece somewhere between 10 percent and 20 percent for their services. This *commission* helps pay for catalog production, publicity, and other business costs.

For years, many auction galleries charged the consignee the full 10 to 20 percent fee. However, this rather steep fee discouraged many people from consigning large collections or high-priced items. In order to encourage business, a large number of galleries are presently adopting a *split-commission* policy. While the gallery continues to command a 20 percent commission, the consignee is charged only 10 percent. The remaining 10 percent is added to the final purchase price of each item auctioned. This, too, is a form of premium charge.

Left and Mail Bids.   A collector or dealer who cannot or does not wish to be present at an auction is often given the opportunity to preview the pieces and leave a bid in writing. If a catalog is available, mail-order bids are also accepted. In both cases, a member of the auctioneer's staff is assigned to act for the absentee bidder. The absentee bidder can often win an item for less than the amount he or she was willing to pay.

Some auction galleries will, if asked to, raise an absentee bid by a small percentage or at least round it out. For example, if absentee bids are made on three toys and the first is overbid, the absentee bid on the second item is automatically raised with the hope that it will win. If this toy is lost too, the absentee bid on the third piece is raised even further. Again, this is done only upon written request. In addition, if the absentee bidder specifically requests, the absentee bid may be rounded off to the next highest amount. For example, if the auction is progressing in graduations of $10, an absentee bid of $35 can be raised to $40 if necessary. If it were not raised in this manner, the person who bid $30 would take the piece even though the absentee bidder had indicated a willingness to pay $5 more.

Telephone Bids.   On occasion, while an auction is in progress the auctioneer may take bids over the telephone from collectors or dealers who could not be present. Whether or not bids are acceptable is up to the discretion of the auctioneer. Because telephone bids can be very disruptive, many galleries will not accept them.

Pieces Bought "As Is."   Remember the time when used-car salesmen could sell cars "as is," before laws were enacted to protect the consumer? Well, so far, there are no laws regulating auctions other than the standards that auctioneers may impose upon themselves. At smaller auction houses, the maxim "Let the buyer beware" still holds true. Usually, pieces are not deliberately misrepresented, but occasionally this does happen. Homework is of the utmost importance. When a bid is made on an item, the assumption is that the collector has looked the item over and is willing to accept it as it stands. Once a piece is sold, the auctioneer is released from his or her responsibility for it unless there is a sizable discrepancy between the description of the piece and its actual condition.

Auctioneer Has Final Say.   It usually goes without saying that if there is any doubt as to the final bidder on an item, the auctioneer will be the determining factor. His or her decision cannot be questioned.

A group of wooden toys produced by the Schoenhut Company of Pennsylvania (ca. 1880s). Included in Schoenhut's line were numerous musical toys, boats, wooden autos, and circus sets. Each of the circus figures pictured has a jointed body, so it could be placed in numerous positions. This innovation led to the Schoenhut Circus's being one of the most popular toys of all time. Illustrated are a few of the figures and animals that comprised the circus sets. Top: a pig, an acrobatic China-man, a ringmaster, a clown, and a lion. Bottom: a goat, a camel, an elephant, and a donkey. RICHARD MERRILL.

Bidding Guidelines

There are a number of common-sense rules to follow when bidding at an auction, especially if you are not accustomed to buying in this manner.

Always get to an auction in plenty of time in order to preview the collection for sale. Bidding wisely on something that you have not examined carefully is very difficult. During the examination of the toys that you may want to purchase, check the following points: Are all the pieces there? Are the colors correct and is the paint original? Has this toy ever been reproduced? Have you ever seen one like it before? Ask yourself these questions before making a commitment.

Once you have decided to make a purchase, try to get a second opinion. Make sure you get an auction or bidding number in order to make sure that you bid on the right toy. Sometimes there will be more than one of a specific toy at an auction. If possible, put your name on the gallery's mailing list.

Check out the competition. Is there anyone there that you recognize? Who is looking "your" toy over? Or, perhaps more importantly, why *isn't* anyone examining that toy? What toys are others interested in and why?

Be careful when bidding. A casual wave to a friend can result in a purchase or, at least, an embarrassing situation. Make sure that the auctioneer knows when you are not bidding.

Remember about the sales tax and the premium charge, if there is one.

Determine what your top bid will be and do not open with that figure. Save it for last. Don't be overanxious.

See how often the crowd opens the bidding at the figure suggested by the auctioneer.

See who is bidding. Is the auctioneer skipping over bids? Do you hear four bids being accepted while only one person appears to be bidding? Again, this is not a common practice, but it occasionally happens.

A grouping of Britains Ltd. railway figures. Included are stationmasters, a flagman, and a signalman. Because they were individually hand-painted, each has a unique facial expression. C. L. COLLINS.

A hobo, redcap, woman, man, and station worker add charm to a toy or train collection. These figures were also produced by Britains Ltd. C. L. COLLINS.

Watch other collectors to see which items they are bidding on and which items they are avoiding. If the auctioneer cannot get even a $10 bid for a toy that should be worth a considerable sum, there is probably a sound reason. Don't be afraid to ask other collectors why they aren't bidding on a particular toy. Even advanced collectors were beginners at one time, and most are more than willing to help.

DEALERS

At some time during your collecting you will interact with antique and toy dealers. You will ask yourself whether these people are reputable or not; whether you should deal with them now or wait; if the price being asked is a fair one; and how you can know that this toy has not been repainted or restored. These and a thousand other questions will come to mind. The answers are to be found through practical experience. Unfortunately, not all dealers or collectors are to be trusted. A few may be genuinely dishonest, while others may simply not know enough about toys to discern a piece's authenticity or true value. Dealers who take advantage of their customers generally do not stay in business for long. To a dealer in general antiques who may have expertise in the fields of furniture and glassware, toys may be out of his or her realm. The field of antiques and collectibles is so large and diverse that knowing everything about it is impossible.

Toy dealers are a special group unto themselves. In addition to buying and selling, many also collect. Often, collectors will become dealers in order to expand their own collections and make the hobby pay for itself. Those toy dealers we know honestly enjoy what they are doing and would not be happy doing anything else. They love the travel, the shows, the people with whom they come in contact, the competition at an auction, and the crazy idea that they are making a living selling second-hand toys.

CHAPTER 3

*S*tarting and *Establishing* *a Collection*

Once a person has become interested in the hobby of collecting antique toys, the first thing he or she will consider is what type of toys to collect. The easiest way out of this dilemma would simply be to start collecting and let nature take its course.

Most beginner's don't take long to decide what types of toys give the most pleasure. Soon after starting to collect old toys, the collector will suddenly realize that the collection includes more banks than tin toys or more tin than cast iron. A preference's being made may be a revelation. The beginner is now a bank (or whatever) collector. Of course, if other attractive toys come along, and they do not happen to be banks, some exceptions will probably be made.

Other collectors take longer to decide the type of toy to acquire. Quite often, they start out trying to amass a large collection of many different types, and they purchase as many toys as quickly as they can. This mode of collecting is the "quantity" method as opposed to the "quality" method. Usually it is only a phase, and once an eye for quality is developed, one type is decided upon. At this time, the collector can get down to the serious business of research and focus all attention and energy in one direction. In this way the collector can become something of an authority in the chosen field. If the collector slowly starts to build a collection, is choosy, and keeps a discriminating eye open as to quality, a large and beautiful collection will grow in only a matter of a few years. Toy collectors have been known to switch their allegiances if they lose interest in the hobby, if toys become scarce, or if prices escalate out of sight. When mechanical banks were easier to come by, there

(Opposite) *A collection of automotive toys. The autos pictured here are mostly of European manufacture and retain the grace and styling reminiscent of the turn-of-the-century runabout.* Top left: *Lehmann's Naughty Boy (Germany, 1912) and Lehmann's OHO, which was also sold under the names ALSO and LOLO about 1912. One example of this toy was sold without a name.* Top right: *Lehmann's AHA Delivery Truck (Germany, 1914).* Middle left: *Bing's Model T (Germany, 1920s).* Middle right: *Bing's DeDion racer (Germany, 1920s).* Bottom left: *Lehmann's TUT TUT, missing the front headlamps (Germany, 1912)* Bottom right: *cast-iron Model A (probably manufactured by the Arcade Company, being filled up by an Arcade gas pump, also cast iron).* RICHARD MERRILL.

were more mechanical-bank collectors. Now that mechanicals have become so costly and hard to find, many collectors are switching to still banks. Similarly, collectors of cast-iron horse-drawn vehicles, toys that have "softened" in value, are now looking for automotive toys and selling their horse-drawn.

Sometimes collectors will purchase toys that will complement other toys in their displays. A train collector, for example, might add some companion pieces, such as vehicles, stations, and people, to the layout, thus creating a *diorama*, a complete scene rather than just a grouping of singular objects.

Many train collectors attempt to amass a collection having at least one model produced by each major toy-train manufacturer. Others may wish to specialize, that is, to try to collect a fair sampling of each type of train made by one manufacturer. To the specialists, variations in locomotives and rolling stock become a matter of key importance and require much research and study. Still other collectors try to collect only trolleys or *department store specials*, trains that were produced by a toy-train manufacturer solely for distribution by a particular department store. Some of the better-known stores, such as

A Bing Budweiser reefer with the word "beer" obliterated in accordance with the United States' prohibition law concerning alcohol. Of special interest to collectors is the fact that this is a standard-gauge car, indicating that it was manufactured specifically for FAO Schwarz, New York City. C. L. COLLINS.

An early Maerklin No. 1-gauge brake van, of special interest to collectors because it was painted especially for the great New York–based toy store, FAO Schwarz (ca. 1898). C. L. COLLINS.

Sears, Macys, FAO Schwarz, and John Wanamaker, each had a train that was produced especially for them. Many of these trains can be identified only by their color scheme, which often was quite different from the common variation of the train being widely distributed.

CLASSIFICATION

There are a number of other good ways to determine what to collect. Some people collect according to the materials used in the production of the toy (wood, tin, cast iron). Others collect by motive power (clockwork, steam, electric, pull toys). Still others collect upon the basis of what the toy represents (trains, airships, trolleys, soldiers, pistols). The possibilities are endless, since within each group there are subgroups and overlapping areas. It is here that some classification problems arise.

Classification can sometimes be a tricky business. What appears on the surface to be a simple matter may cause hot debate between different factions of collectors. A case in point is the Main Street Trolley bank. It can be correctly classified as a still bank and is found in bank collections. The toy is also a trolley car and so will be found in some trolley-car collections. It is also a cast-iron toy and, since the wheels turn, it can also be considered a pull toy. Some train collectors consider this bank to be a train-related item, since trolleys are the transition piece between the horse, the train, and the automobile.

All of these collectors are right in their viewpoints, and each would probably argue that the piece correctly belongs in his or her collection. The final decision ultimately rests with the individual collector. Don't be afraid, then, of purchasing toys that overlap categories. They quite often add an extra bit of charm that serves to enhance a good toy collection. New vistas of the toy world are open to those who pioneer and experiment in new areas.

Ignored to a great extent are the folk-art, handmade toys, many of which were one of a kind. The majority of collectors primarily seek toys that were products of mass production and can be traced to a specific maker. While symbolic of the early days of the machine age, these old toys reflect the craftsmanship and beauty of form and design that is characteristic of the early 1900s.

A cast-iron coupe (ca. 1915–1920), desired by many bank collectors because of its rarity. The auto pictured is painted red, has nickled, spoked wheels, and is a floor toy as well as a bank. The near-mint condition of this toy adds to its value and desirability. C. L. COLLINS.

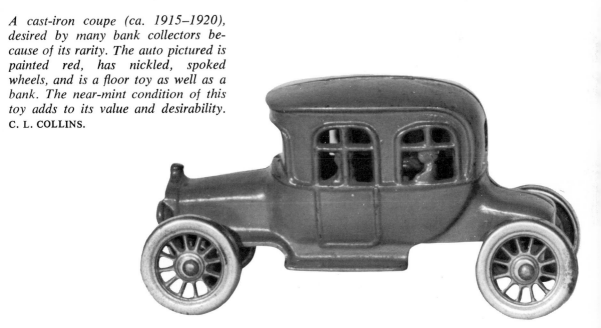

ORIGINAL SOURCE MATERIALS

Old Catalogs and Paraphernalia

If you are to become fully involved in the hobby of toy collecting, research will be of the utmost importance. Historical information (such as manufacturer and original materials), color schemes, size, and price are all fascinating as well as essential bits of information that can be discovered while browsing through old manufacturers' catalogs, the best possible source of information. Through the use of catalogs, the researchers can trace the history of the toy industry in the United States from its infancy, the development of a

A 1908 Edmonds-Metzel train catalog. The page shown illustrates the deluxe engine and large passenger cars together with the simpler locomotive and less expensive smaller lithographed Pullman cars. C. L. COLLINS.

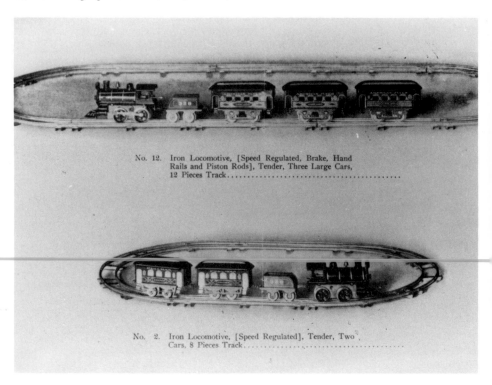

No. 12. Iron Locomotive, [Speed Regulated, Brake, Hand Rails and Piston Rods], Tender, Three Large Cars, 12 Pieces Track...

No. 2. Iron Locomotive, [Speed Regulated], Tender, Two Cars, 8 Pieces Track...

specific toy or toy type over a period of years, and the major as well as minor changes in materials, construction, design, and packaging.

Most of the better books written specifically about collecting model trains are out of print and considered collector items themselves. But original or reproduced manufacturers' catalogs can provide a wealth of information about what models and accessories were produced in what year, which line of cars accompanied a specific engine, and what changes were made in the production of certain items from one year to the next. Keep in mind that manufacturers sometimes pictured proposed models that never actually reached the production or assembly stage, and that many special department-store lines seldom appeared in conventional catalogs. By comparing catalogs one can see how manufacturers "borrowed" ideas from one another or produced toys so similar that the toys can be mistaken for one another. For example, note the similarities between the early locomotive cars produced by Ives and Maerklin. Who copied from whom is not really important. Collectors have more fun when they can accuse one company or the other and argue among themselves. Then, as now, industrial espionage was common and profitable, and the enforcement of copyright and patent laws was more lax during the last century. And despite a belief to the contrary, not all early American toys were copies of European models. Quite often the reverse was true. There was a booming toy business in the United States as early as the late 1860s, and many European toy manu-

Look-alikes. The early Maerklin passenger car on the left closely resembles an Ives car of approximately the same period (1901). Both are hand-painted, are embossed on the bodies and over the windows, and have cast-iron wheels. C. L. COLLINS.

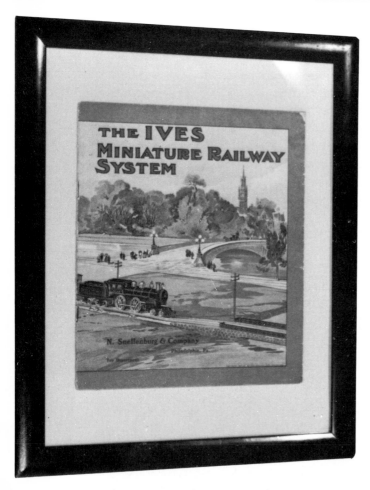

A framed Ives toy-train catalog from 1908. Here it is used as a train-room accent piece. C. L. COLLINS.

facturers copied toys that were produced here and then sold their copies on the American market. Examining the claims of superiority made by competing manufacturers is interesting. Manufacturers quite often indulged in such comparisons and boasted that their own products could perform Herculean feats.

From old catalogs you can also learn which toys were popular for a sustained period and which toys were popular for only a short time. For example, the Tammany bank and the Owl bank were very popular among children and so were manufactured for about forty years, while the ornate Palace bank, manufactured by the Ives Company, was produced for only a few years. Owing to this fact, the Palace bank is a much rarer piece and is a welcome addition to any collection, even though it is a still bank and the others are mechanicals.

In addition to their historic and reference value, old catalogs possess their own charm and aesthetic appeal. They are collectible antiques in themselves. A number of collectors have been known to frame and display old catalogs in order to accent their collections. Framed box covers, especially the older lithographed ones, are also a decorative addition.

Old catalogs, like old toys, are getting harder and harder to locate as the demand has grown for these original source materials. To meet this demand, facsimiles are being printed. Despite their research value, they lack the charm of the originals, which one imagined were waited for and purchased by a child, to be lovingly studied and then carefully stored for further reference.

Advertising Materials

Old catalogs are only one of the many original reference sources available to an energetic collector. Most toy companies sent out fliers that announced new toys and toy lines. Though as hard if not harder to find as catalogs, fliers are a handy supplementary research tool.

Easier to locate are advertisements in old newspapers and magazines. Though not very complete, advertisements usually gave a description of the toy, the approximate date of manufacture, possibly the manufacturers' name, and the selling price.

Fliers and advertisements are attractive when framed and are of value to

A complete set of advertising stamps issued by the Ives Company (1916–1917).
C. L. COLLINS.

collectors of advertising memorabilia as well as to toy collectors. This is also true of any type of advertising material that included a company's name, such as letters, documents, cards, pencils, calendars, advertising displays, and signs.

Trade Cards

When each mechanical bank was boxed by a manufacturer, it was accompanied by a trade card. On this card was a drawing of the bank, a description of colors and size, a list of operating instructions, an explanation of the expected results, the manufacturer's name, and the price. Trade cards are now prized collector's items and are quite often displayed as complementary pieces to a bank collection.

The most common trade cards are those that were printed by the Sheppard Hardware Company and the J. E. Stevens Company. The more desirable Sheppard cards are colored lithographs printed on heavy, quality paper. The cards printed by Stevens are usually pale blue, brown, or white and are of

An Ives box top (1902–1903). Such a piece adds color and flavor to any collection room. C. L. COLLINS.

poorer quality. They are nonetheless charming, appealing, and collectible. Stevens cards are easier to find than Sheppard cards and are usually affordable (under $12). Sheppard cards usually bring at least twice that amount.

Boxes

Yet another type of source material that makes an interesting addition to any toy collection is an original box. An appealing old toy seems to be even more so when found in its original box. It makes the toy just that much more complete and shows how much the toy was valued by its original owner. Under no circumstances, then, should an original box be discarded and just the toy saved, regardless of the condition of the box. Remember, the more complete a toy is, the more valuable it is for research or resale. Collectors will generally pay a premium for a toy if it is still in its original box, especially if the box is a beautifully lithographed one made before 1920.

We have found that the best way to preserve a fragile cardboard box is to store it in a cool, dry place. If feasible, place the cardboard box inside a wooden one with a glass cover that encloses and frames the original box. Be sure that no harmful condensation can form on the underside of the glass. Stored this way, the old box becomes an unusual conversation piece.

If the box is slightly ripped or the seams are split, sew it with heavy thread that matches the color of the box. Most collectors would rather have a box that has been sewn back together than one that has been taped. Tape tends to discolor and crack, and if it is not applied properly, it can tear the box even further.

You can see, then, that printed matter of the types described is eagerly sought after for its research and aesthetic value. When used as reference tools, these materials are enlightening; when used for display purposes, they add an extra bit of charm to enhance and complement any toy collection.

PROTECTING A COLLECTION

Unfortunately, theft is a problem to collectors, even toy collectors. Antiques are fairly easy to dispose of, and toys are no exception. Our intention is not to needlessly panic anyone but to simply alert collectors to this very real danger. There are several precautions that collectors can take.

Antitheft devices have proven effective in preventing or at least hindering an intruder's access to a collection. Although any type of burglar alarm system may be expensive, such devices do provide peace of mind. If collectors have sizable collections at home and advertise that they are collectors, there is a chance that the wrong person may see the ad. Collectors are wise to speak with an insurance agent. A collection can never really be replaced once it is stolen, but there is some comfort in knowing that at least it is insured.

Several organizations, including the Train Collectors Association, have

An American Flyer catalog cover (1914). Although this example is lithographed in black and white, brightly colored ones were also available at this time. C. L. COLLINS.

Below: *This page from the American Flyer catalog of 1914 shows the European accessories used and sold by American Flyer at the time.* C. L. COLLINS.

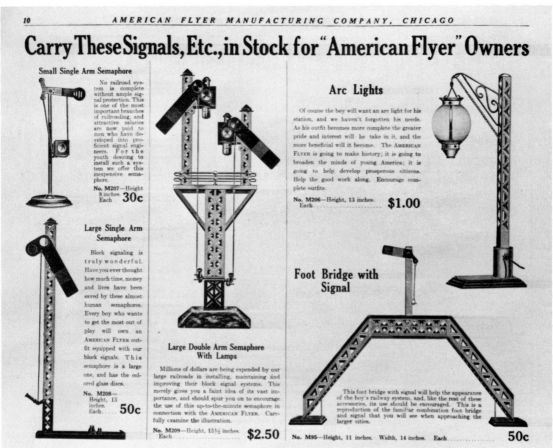

formed a sort of brotherhood to protect the interests of their members. If there is a theft, lists of the stolen toys are publicized and made available to the entire membership. In this way collectors can keep an eye out for stolen toys that may appear at a show or an auction. If a piece's ownership is questionable, the seller and the FBI are notified, and in this way toys are sometimes recovered.

DISPLAYING AND CARING FOR A COLLECTION

Once a toy collection has been started, a decision must be made regarding the proper means of housing, displaying, and caring for it. The final decision will be based on the individual collector's wants and needs as well as on his or her finances and space limitations.

The majority of collectors tend to set aside one area that has been specifically designated the "collection room." This may be a finished attic, a basement, a den, or a garage, in which the bulk of the collection will be stored. The collector will then choose a suitable manner of displaying individual pieces within the collection.

Many toy enthusiasts seem to prefer to display their collections on wooden shelves, which are attached to the walls and usually evenly spaced

A tantalizing shelving display of early O-gauge toy trains by Ives (ca. 1900–1911).
C. L. COLLINS.

from ceiling to floor. This form of display is convenient in that it efficiently uses the available space and at the same time offers unobstructed viewing. Many items of varying size can be displayed in this manner. Most train collections are displayed in this fashion. The shelving is often grooved according to the gauge of the train to be displayed. The wheels of the engines and cars fit snugly in these grooves, thereby preventing slippage and accidental breakage. Other train collections are displayed on track, which is sometimes secured to the shelves by tacks or nails. In this way the trains are displayed in a natural setting, yet the track won't slide off the shelf.

The use of shelving can be a highly effective method of displaying toys, trains, or banks, but all too often the shelves are placed so close together that the overall charm of the collection is entirely lost. Individual pieces lose their identity, and the collection takes on a cluttered appearance. Although some space is lost when the shelves are moderately separated, the lost space is more than compensated for by the overall effect of the display. Each item can be

An American Flyer lithographed box top (1914), protected by a custom-made, glass-front box. C. L. COLLINS.

clearly seen and thus receives the full attention of the viewer. We believe that of all the collections we have visited, those that were displayed spaciously and simplistically were by far the most pleasing.

Other individuals prefer to display their collections behind protective glass enclosures. Bookcases, china and knickknack cabinets, and drugstore and department-store cases are only a few of the numerous items used to display collections. These enclosures offer protection from dust and dirt, yet they may obstruct the viewing of individual items.

There are still other collectors who prefer not to display their collection in one specific room. Instead, they use their toys as decorative or accent pieces. Such items can be displayed on a mantel or coffee table, used as bookends, or mounted on a wall in place of conventional pictures. Such techniques, if carefully planned, can be a pleasurable and highly effective means of displaying a collection.

Once the collector has established where and how his or her collection is to be kept, some thought should be given to lighting. Direct sunlight can cause quick deterioration of a toy's finish and should be avoided as a primary light source. Most collectors seem to prefer to use of fluorescent lighting, as it is very economical and tends to enhance many of the toys' vivid color schemes. Other collectors use sophisticated lighting techniques, such as illuminated cases, ceiling panel lights, and recessed spots, which focus the viewer's attention on specific "prized" items.

Another equally important consideration when designing a collection room is how to control the room's humidity. A high degree of humidity can be disastrous to antique toys. Castiron will rust, paint will flake, nickel will pit, and tin will mold. Although boxes of baking soda and bags of silica gel can absorb moisture, we recommend that the serious collector consider purchasing a dehumidifier. While this is rather costly, it is probably the most efficient means of effectively controlling humidity, and thus protecting what could be a sizable investment.

In addition to the consideration given to the display of a collection, the collector should give an equal amount of attention to the care and cleaning of the toys themselves.

Very few of us are able to acquire toys in their original factory condition. Over the years, toys were subjected to much use and abuse at the hands of their youthful owners. Often they were stored for years in damp cellars or kept in musty attics. Thus, the majority of toys found today need some form of repair in order to restore them to nearly their original condition.

Many collectors are afraid to service their toys in fear of damaging them further. There are, however, many ways of safely improving the appearance of old toys. If an old toy is found to be extremely dirty, a mild soap-and-water solution may be all that is necessary to dramatically improve its condition. A solution of one part baking soda to five parts water or a mild dish-washing detergent is especially effective for removing dirt and film from paint and lithography. A strong detergent or cleanser is not wise to use, as it may cause old paint to discolor, run, or fade.

Once a toy has been thoroughly cleaned, a light coating of oil or liquid wax should be applied. It will protect and enhance the finish for years to come.

Although most collectors avoid purchasing broken toys, such items are useful for the parts that can be salvaged. However, if a rare toy is found in broken condition, it may be worth having restored. Many mechanical toys are difficult to repair. A serious break in the casting of an iron toy greatly reduces its value. There are, however, professionals who are skilled in repairing such defects. If a toy merits being repaired, these people can be relied upon to do an excellent job.

No matter how you decide to house or display a collection of antique toys, there is little doubt that with proper care it will provide many years of enjoyment not only for the owner but also for all those privileged to see it.

SELLING

If you have some old toys you have decided to sell but don't know where or for how much, show the toys to several dealers. Do not sell them to the first person who makes you an offer. You might consider researching the toys in a price guide. Although price guides are not completely accurate, they provide rough estimates of the values. Also, try to find the names of collectors and antique dealers in your area.

A dirty or dusty toy is not necessarily worth a fortune, and a rusty toy is not necessarily old. Usually, just the opposite is true. Many part-time dealers and new collectors are apparently unaware of these simple facts, as evidenced by the prices that some dealers attempt to charge and some collectors are willing to pay for a worthless toy.

If you have some idea of your toys' worth, setting up at a flea market and trying to sell the toys yourself may be fun. Select a flea market that caters to antiques (rather than plumbing supplies) and you may do well. At the very least, the experience will be a new and interesting one for you. Maybe you too will "get the bug" and become a collector or dealer in the fascinating world of antique toys.

CHAPTER 4

Toys in America

In this chapter we take a glimpse at the history of the American toy industry, a topic that would take a number of volumes to treat with justice. Tracing the birth of the toy industry is somewhat impossible, since many, if not most, old records have been lost through indifference or natural calamities, such as fire. Unfortunately, the complete and true story of where the first toys were manufactured and mass-produced in this country will probably never be known.

Some evidence indicates, however, that the second half of the eighteenth century is a good place to look for the roots of the toy industry. During this period, at the onset of the Industrial Revolution, numerous tin and glass manufacturers began to realize a potential market for children's toys. This potential market was finally reached in a very tangible way during the mid-1800s, at about the time of the Civil War. We will be primarily concerned with the manufacturers who were in business starting with the 1860s, since few earlier toys exist in any number. Amazingly, many toys from the 1860s and 1870s do exist, and they are favorites among many collectors. They are the ones that will receive our main attention.

Before 1860, the United States was still fairly well caught up in the Puritan work ethic, and play was thought to be nonproductive. To be successful, one had to work every day and save one's hard-earned money. Since no laws were in effect to protect children, they were forced to work alongside adults. Children were considered to be miniature adults and were treated as such. In fact, until the late 1860s, toys were usually used to teach moral lessons rather than to divert children. For example, the common practice on Sundays was to allow children to play only with toys that would teach biblical history, such as Noah's Arks.

Although the idea of toys purely for the sake of amusement was a somewhat foreign notion to the steadfast Yankee of the early 1800s, it had caught

One of a series of herald cars by the Hafner Company (1919). This car was specially finished in red, white, and blue, and bears the herald of the Toy Manufacturers of the USA, Inc. C. L. COLLINS.

on by the 1860s and had catapulted a number of toy manufacturers to prominence. Children were finally going to be allowed to be children and the market was there for the asking. And, it was during this period that many of the big names in the toy business got their start.

CARD GAMES AND BOARD GAMES

The card games and board games that appeared in the 1850s and 1860s would be considered quite boring by today's standards. One of the most popular board games was the Mansion of Happiness, considered by many collectors to be the first board game published in the United States. Mansion was published by the W. S. & B. Ives Company of Salem, Massachusetts, in 1843. Similar to the French game of Goose, Mansion was a chase game in which the players vied with one another to get to the center of the board first. At every stop along the way the players confronted the virtues of honesty, justice, piety, and truth, as well as the pitfalls of humanity, immodesty, idleness, cruelty, and perjury, which led one eventually to the stocks and pillory and finally to prison and ruination. Although it was not an especially pleasant game, Mansion was so popular that when Parker Brothers took over the Ives Company, it released its own version in the 1880s. The later Parker Brothers version is the one most often found today. The earlier version by Ives, which was hand-colored and lithographed, is a much rarer find, but such finds still do occur.

WOODEN TOYS

Although many collectors would disagree, we believe that wooden toys are a too often ignored group. With very few exceptions, such as trolleys, trains, doll houses (especially by Bliss), and fire engines, this group has been generally overlooked for too long. The wooden toys that appear at auction tend to bring prices far lower than their tin and cast-iron counterparts. With this being the case, wooden toys might be a good field with which to become involved. A person who was knowledgeable in this area could perhaps amass an impressive collection before prices reached those realized by the other groups.

The Pacific (ca. late 1870s). Called a "grand excursion train to the Rocky Mountains and California," the Pacific was made of wood and covered with lithographed paper. It was manufactured by the W. S. Reed Company of Leominister, Massachusetts. The train is in its original condition and, when put together, makes a very impressive display piece. Note the lettering on each car: "This is the car in which good little girls and boys may ride." RICHARD MERRILL.

With their manufacture dating to before the Civil War, wooden toys are probably the oldest mass-produced group; and despite their homemade appearance, most of these early toys were manufactured in factories. Probably one of the most popular of the wooden toys is the Noah's Ark. Many of these "Sunday toys" were quite elaborate for this era, which was known for its simplistic life style, and could carry up to one hundred pairs of animals as well as Noah and his family. Again, during the 1850s and 1860s, when toys were frowned upon, children were allowed to play only with this toy on Sunday. As a result, Noah and his family were able to escape the flood at least once a week.

From the time of the Civil War to the early 1900s, any toy that could be produced in tin or cast iron had its counterpart in wood. The colorful lithographed paper that was pasted on the sides of wooden toys allowed them to be far more detailed than many of the tin and cast-iron examples. Boats and trains, street cars and fire engines, circus wagons and castles, all were produced in wood. Many of these toys, especially the boats and fire engines, are rare today. Others, like bowling sets, blocks, and construction sets, are more common.

The Bliss Manufacturing Company of Rhode Island helped pave the way for wooden toys with colorfully lithographed paper sides. It was a very prolific firm that produced almost every conceivable type of wooden toy, but it is most noted for its colorful doll houses. Also of note are its fire engines, paddle boats, and trains. Until recently, however, wooden toys by Bliss and other manufacturers had a limited following. Only within the past ten years or so has Bliss become a household name with collectors.

One of the largest producers of wooden toys was the firm of Crandall. From the 1880s to the early 1900s, large quantities of wooden toys poured out from about ten Crandall factories located in Pennsylvania and New York. Included in the inventory were the Acrobats, Expression Blocks, Sectional ABC Blocks, Masquerade Blocks, Building Blocks, District School, Lively Horseman, Velocipede and Rider, Happy Family, Performing Animals, and Donkey and Rider.

Especially noteworthy are Crandall's animated toys and those that were produced as a single unit (as opposed to a boxed set which had numerous components). Complete boxed sets are difficult to find but worth the effort. Most Crandall toys, even the earlier ones, were accurately marked and can be easily identified. This marking is, of course, of great advantage to the researcher/collector.

Other manufacturers of wooden toys included the Reed Company, noted for the fine lithography used on its trains and trolley cars; the Milton Bradley Company, noted for its extensive line of wooden toys, puzzles, and board games; the Gibbs Manufacturing Company, noted for its walking horse and

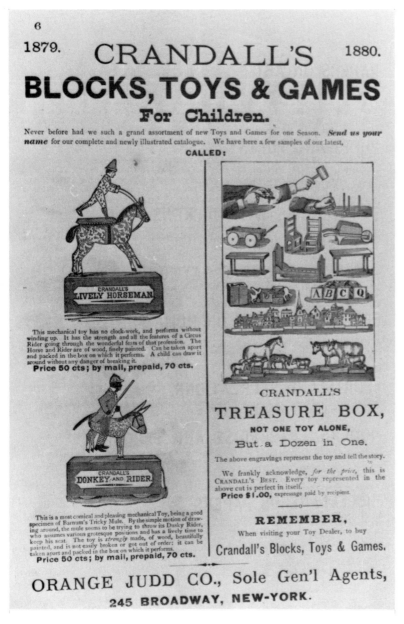

An advertisement by the Orange Judd Company, New York, for its line of wooden toys manufactured by Crandall (1879–1881). Illustrated are Crandall's Lively Horseman, and Donkey and Rider, which are rarer than the Treasure Box, also illustrated. RICHARD MERRILL.

wagon; and the McLoughlin Brothers, most noted for the marvelous lithography used on its toys and box covers. Many collectors have bought a boxed toy by McLoughlin, even if most of the parts were missing, just for the box itself.

Of all the companies and toys mentioned, the wooden toys that have the largest following among collectors include the trains, ferry boats, circus wagons, fire engines, and puzzles.

An early Milton Bradley jigsaw puzzle (1860), designed to teach children the component parts of a locomotive. C. L. COLLINS.

As with other toys, wooden toys have not escaped the hand of the forger. Try to know your toys before making a purchase; wooden toys are easy to fake.

TIN TOYS

The tin-toy industry in this country can be traced with some degree of certainty to the 1840s and perhaps even earlier. At that time, the production of tin toys was a cottage industry. Early tinsmiths, realizing the potential toy market, began to create toys from the scraps left over from a day's work. They had to be content with making toys as the demand presented itself, until the 1860s when the market for manufactured toys justified the formation of companies devoted solely to the production of toys. Tin toys started to replace the handmade and factory-produced wooden toys. Within a few short years the tin-toy industry in this country was in full bloom.

Surprisingly, tin toys have only recently come into their own as a desirable group to collect. Names like George Brown of Connecticut (active from 1850 to 1889); James Fallows of Pennsylvania (1890s); Francis, Field & Francis of New York (1850s and 1860s); and Althof Bergmann of New York (1860s) have become legendary and stand for the best of the American tin toys. These companies' products were made with such love and care for detail that they are every bit as attractive today as they were one hundred years ago.

Even though an untrained eye often has difficulty identifying a toy as having been made by one of these manufacturers, just the style and charm of an old tin toy makes it worth buying.

Another manufacturer of note, though not as prolific as some of the others, was Jerome Secor of Bridgeport, Connecticut. Secor started as a clock-maker in about 1860. As a sideline he manufactured a few toys, the most important of which are his fine clockwork figures. The Freedman's Bank, probably one of the rarest of all mechanical banks, was made by Secor in response to President Lincoln's freeing of the slaves. It has a black, cloth-dressed figure, seated behind what appears to be a table, in front of whom the depositor can place a coin. The bank, since it is a clockwork, can be wound up. When it is, a lever is depressed to trigger the action. The figure's left hand sweeps the coin into a slot, while his right hand rises as he "thumbs his nose" at the depositor. Only a few examples of this highly sought bank are known to have survived, probably because of the high initial cost of the bank. During the 1860s the toy retailed for about $5, quite an exorbitant sum for the time.

Secor used the same figure in another clockwork toy of his, the Banjo Player. When wound, the player appears to play his instrument. But probably the most popular toy that Secor produced was a simple singing bird that

A combination tin, cast-iron, and wood locomotive stenciled with the bold name Eagle. Manufactured by the George W. Brown Company of Forestville, Connecticut (1856), this is a very fine example of a rare toy. RICHARD MERRILL.

A collection of early American tin toys. During the past few years, there has been a virtual renaissance of interest in early tin toys, especially American and German examples. Pictured is a sampling of the type of toys that are capturing the hearts of so many collectors. Top left: *a walking-girl platform toy, probably manufactured by the Althof Bergmann Company of New York (1870s).* Top right: *a tiger platform toy.* Middle left: *an early Gong Bell Company (ca. 1870) tin-horse bell toy. The bell and wheels are cast iron.* Middle right: *a trotting-horse platform toy, possibly by the George Brown Company of Connecticut (1870s).* Bottom: *a horse-drawn streetcar, or omnibus, probably by Hull & Stafford of Clinton, Connecticut (1860–1870s). An interesting point to note is the size of the horses in comparison to the streetcar. No attention to proportion was made at all, which, of course, adds to the charm of the toy.* RICHARD MERRILL.

worked like a whistle when placed in the spout of a kettle. This toy was so popular that copies are being manufactured even today.

Many of Secor's toys were distributed by another toy maker from Bridge-port, one of the most legendary of them all, Edward Ives. The Ives Company (not to be confused with the W. S. & B. Ives Company of Salem, Massachusetts) was founded in the 1860s, and within thirty years it had become one of the largest and most important dealerships in the world. After the death of Edward, his son Harry took control of the firm. Under Harry's leadership, the Ives Railway Line (Ives is probably better known for trains than other toys) graduated from clockwork to electric and went through a multiplicity of styles and variations. Discussion of Ives trains alone could fill an entire book.

Through several name changes (Edward Ives Co.; Ives, Blakeslee & Co.; Ives, Blakeslee & Williams; Ives Manufacturing Co.), a few changes of address, and a devastating fire, the Ives firm continued for over seventy years with its straightforward and honest approach to manufacturing nothing but the best toys. But for a number of reasons—its refusal to compromise quality, its unprecedented generosity to small clients, and its failure in a line of boats that was manufactured as a patriotic gesture to promote the merchant marine—the company was forced out of business during the 1930s. Lionel and a few other companies bought up what remained of the prestigious firm of Ives. To this

The King, manufactured by the Ives Company as one of the Ives fleet of boats (ca. 1923–1925). This clockwork toy is wound by inserting the key in the smoke-stack. Below, the waterline is painted red while the area above is painted black. The deck is tan, the cabin section a darker brown. The mast, which is located in front of the cabin, is missing on this particular example. C. L. COLLINS.

The Ives Navy. During the early 1900s, the Ives Company of Bridgeport, Connecticut, embarked on a new toy-line venture that would, in part, be a contributing factor to its bankruptcy in the mid-1930s. The secretary of the navy was urging toy companies to help promote the establishment of a new branch of military service, the Merchant Marine. The secretary believed that the introduction and marketing of a fleet of toy boats would help introduce this new concept to the public, in general, and to children, in particular. What the secretary was looking for was public approval. Unfortunately for Ives, the idea did not work out that way. The boat line that was introduced in 1916 and carried until 1930 was not as popular as had been expected and Ives lost a great deal of money each year it was carried. But, being a good and patriotic American, Harry Ives kept the line going. The government, strangely enough, would not offer to help subsidize the company when it became apparent that it was in trouble, and so the Ives Company disappeared. Since the Ives fleet was not popular, their boats are somewhat difficult to locate today, especially those in good condition. Those that were sold were apparently played with a great deal. The boat pictured is the Sally, which is approximately 12 inches long. The area below the waterline is painted green while the rest of the boat is painted tan and dark brown. The smokestacks are red. The boat is powered by a clockwork mechanism hidden in the hull. The key shaft is located inside the smokestack, and the boat is shown with the original key. RICHARD MERRILL.

day the Ives saying "Ives Toys Make Happy Boys" holds true. Only now we substitute "Collectors" for "Boys."

So many tin toys were produced during the 1850s and 1860s that it is amazing that more of the early toys have not survived. However, those that

An Ives No. 115 freight station (1906). Note the lithographed roof, doors, and base. This model has tin nameplates and a cast-iron chimney top.

An Ives No. 114 passenger station (1906) with cast-iron door and window inserts. Ives excelled in the intricacy of its lithographed designs.

An Ives No. 115 freight station (1908–1910). This building is entirely lithographed, as opposed to the painted 1906 version.

A Maerklin freight station (1900–1910). Similar to the Ives freight stations, this model is finished in a pebbly, stuccolike material. The Maerkin trademark is stamped on the base.

An Ives No. 114 passenger station (1908–1910). Identical in design to the 1906 model, this station is lithographed in a creamy wood-grained finish. Notice that the separate tin office sign of the 1906 model has been replaced by one incorporated directly into the lithography.

An Ives No. 113 passenger station (1910). Although this station retains the early cast-iron chimney top and the door and window inserts, the separate lithographed nameplate has been dropped.

n Ives No. 115 freight station (1911). This station represents an entirely new design for the Ives cessories. Beginning in 1911, Ives completely discontinued the use of sliding doors and cast-iron *im. Buildings were then "realistically" finished with simulated interior and exterior details. If you ok closely, you can observe the shadow of the scale lithographed on the wall as well as the name es on the box being transported by the worker.*

An Ives No. 17 clockwork engine atop a No. 146 automatic turntable (1904). The top of the table is wound and secured by the brass lever on the right. When released, the internal clockwork mechanism automatically brings the engine to the next track position.

A lithographed Ives No. 126 caboose (1906– 1909).

*An Ives No. 61 Empress passenger car (1906).
Note the beautiful lithography and hand-painted roof.*

An Ives clockwork motor boat (1923–1925). Named Vim, this was only one of seven power boats in the Ives fleet.

An Ives No. 3239 No. 1-gauge electric locomotive (1920). Usually found in black, this is an extremely rare variation. Probably repainted at the Ives factory, this 3239 is finished in the same brown usually assigned to standard-gauge engines.

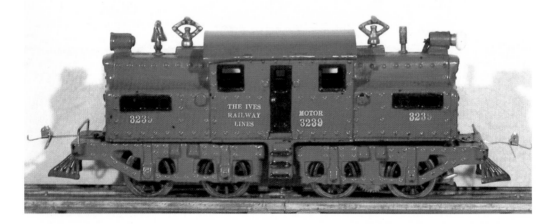

*American Miniature Railway Company cast-iron No. 20 locomotive
and tender (1909). Produced by two former Ives employees, this engine
bears a striking similarity to the Ives products of the same period.*

*A small Edmonds-Metzel passenger car (1907). Perhaps one of the
earliest cars produced by this firm, it bears the words Pullman
and Chicago. The beautiful lithography includes simulated doors and windows.*

A large series Edmonds-Metzel passenger car (1907–1908). American Flyer was used as a road name; the true American Flyer Company was not founded until 1910. Note that the windows and doors are punched out.

A later Edmonds-Metzel American Flyer passenger car (1910). These beautiful little cars are found with both true Metzel engines and early Flyer locomotives.

Opposite: *A section of shelving in a collection room. Thoug, the shelves are rather closely spaced, the trains displayed ca, be clearly viewed. From top to bottom, the trains shown are*

Karl Bub clockwork passenger set (ca. 1910–1912)
Ives clockwork passenger set (ca. 1906)
Girard "Joy Line" clockwork freight set (ca. 1930)
Ives clockwork freight set (ca. 1912)
Dorfan electric freight set (ca. 1920)
American Flyer Hummer electric freight set (ca. 1928)
American Flyer electric freight set (ca. 1925)
Hafner passenger set (ca. 1925)

An Ives No. 801 clockwork trolley (1910).

A Bing snowplow (mid-1920s). As it was pushed along in front of a locomotive, a spring attached to the front wheels caused the blades to rotate in a realistic manner.

A cast-iron Yellow Cab bank (ca. 1925). Manufactured by the Arcade Company, this piece was produced as a toy and a bank. Both 4-inch and 7½-inch sizes.

A Daisy Bell toy (1893). It was manufactured by the Gong Bell Company.

A Puritan paddle-wheeler (1903). It was manufactured by the Harris Company.

*A cast-iron Yellow Cab toy (1920). Manufactured by the Arcade Company,
this is one toy that most collectors like to have in their collection.*

An early Gong Bell toy (ca. 1880). A simple rolling gong bell is attached to a small tin horse. The toy is 6 inches long.

An early tin horse-drawn wagon (late 1870). It was possibly manufactured in Europe. Note the unusual stamped-tin wheels.

*Three figural still banks (1900–1910). The Boy Scout and Sailor
were probably manufactured by A. C. Williams. Also shown is a chubby
Civil War character with "Give Billy a Penny" embossed on his chest.*

*A Puppy Dog with Bee still bank and a cute complementary
piece—a Puppy Dog with Bee lamp (1920).*

A group of fairly common animal still banks: Cat with Bowtie, Seated Monkey, Sitting Bulldog, and Goose. All are made of cast-iron except the Monkey, which is cast in brass. The most numerous group among the still banks is that of animals (1910–1920).

A Tammany bank (ca. 1875). Manufactured by the J. E. Stevens Company, Tammany was one of the most popular mechanical banks of all. It was produced for over forty years and thus is very easily found.

An Owl on Stump mechanical bank (1880s). As common as the Tammany bank, it is found just as easily. It was also manufactured by the J. E. Stevens Company for forty years.

A Speaking Dog bank (1885). It was manufactured first in the 1880s by the Sheppard Hardware Company and later by the J. E. Stevens Company. Although the casting is the same, the paint quality on the later Stevens version is superior to that of the earlier Sheppard one.

An Eagle and Eaglets bank (1886). Manufactured by the J. E. Stevens Company, it is a favorite among collectors. Put a penny in the mother eagle's beak and press the lever, and mother feeds her youngsters. A fine action bank with a true American theme.

A Professor Pug Frog's
Great Bicycle Feat bank
(1880s). Place a penny in
front of the rear wheel,
wind up the pedal, and
release the lever near
Mother Goose's arm. The
Professor does a com-
plete somersault, deposit-
ing the penny with the
clown. Manufactured by
the J. E. Stevens Com-
pany.

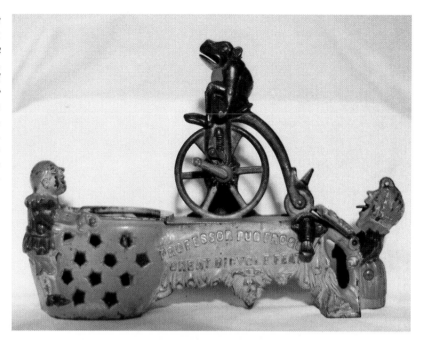

A Punch and Judy mechanical bank
(ca. 1884). Manufactured by the
Sheppard Hardware Company,
it was a favorite with children.

A Penny Pineapple mechanical bank (1960).
One of the new mechanical banks, it was
manufactured in honor of the admittance of
Hawaii to the Union in 1959. Finely cast in
iron, this is a fine bank to add to a collection.
Only the first 500 banks were cast with the
date July 4, 1960.

A Teddy and the Bear bank (1903). The bank pictured shows the completed action. Teddy (Roosevelt) shoots a penny into the tree, thus triggering the bear to spring out of the top. It was manufactured by the J. E. Stevens Company.

A Trick Pony bank (1885). It is a beautiful equestrian bank. When a penny is placed in the pony's mouth and the lever is depressed, the pony bows and deposits the coin in the water trough. Difficult to find in good original condition, the Trick Pony was manufactured by Sheppard Hardware Company.

were durable enough to survive and remain totally intact are very difficult to attribute to and authenticate as being from a specific date and manufacturer. This difficulty arises from a lack of manufacturers' catalogs and other original source material. Only an experienced eye is able to assign one of these earlier toys to a specific maker with any amount of accuracy. One of the few ways that a novice can tell if a toy is from this earlier period is by examining the wheels on the pull toys. The earlier wheels were almost always cast iron and very primitive in appearance and feel. The chances of finding one of these toys is somewhat slim, but one never knows.

Amazing things do happen in this hobby, as illustrated by the recent discovery, near Hartford, Connecticut, of the original sketchbook of George Brown. Brown is legendary among collectors of early American tin toys. His firm produced fine-quality tin toys during the 1850s and 1860s and was later absorbed into the Stevens & Brown Company. The sketches discovered were a group of working drawings and designs for toys that were to be produced by Brown. Also shown in the sketchbook are changes in toy designs and outright rejections of certain toys. This discovery will prove an invaluable link for the serious tin-toy collector and historian to a previously lost era. The sketchbook has been reproduced and is available to collectors. Unfortunately, discoveries like this one are rare.

The most readily found early tin toys were manufactured in the period from 1860 to 1890 and are as diverse as any of the other groups that we will mention. Tin horses pulling wagons; fire engines; trains with impressive-sounding names such as Union, Challenge, and Victor stenciled across their boilers; steamboats; animals on wheels; complete kitchens (sometimes equipped with a working water pump); and horses in hoops were among the many toys that lined the shop shelves at Christmastime during the heyday of tin-toy production.

It was not unusual, during the late 1860s and 1870s, for toy factories to turn out tin toys by the tens of millions. Some records show that forty to fifty million toys per factory per year is not an exaggerated figure. One wonders, then, where did they all go? Scrap-metal drives or whatever? The question is best answered by posing another question: How many of the toys that you played with as a child do you still have? They were just toys, right? Luckily for the collector, some toys were saved or at least put away in attics and forgotten about until later.

Tin-toy collecting is a somewhat enigmatic hobby. It is both exciting and frustrating at the same time. At every turn one runs into obstacles, such as the lack of original documents and of marked toys (most were not). Then there are the breakthroughs, such as the discovery of George Brown's sketchbook. But regardless of the problems, or maybe because of them, tin-toy collecting is a rewarding field and also a relatively safe one, in that there seem to be fewer

reproductions than in other areas. To reproduce tin toys, one would need a costly arrangement of tools and dies, stamping machines, and other equipment. In contrast, cast-iron reproduction requires only a pail and sand and some molten metal. The almost prohibitive cost of reproducing tin toys has kept the tin-toy hobby fairly clean, and this fact, in turn, has added many new followers, including some former collectors of cast iron.

The problems with tin rest in composites, missing parts, and manufacturer identification. *Composites,* a problem in all areas of toy collecting, are toys that were put together by using parts from other toys. They were never produced as that completed toy; they are fantasy toys and they have no real value other than for parts. Discovering that a toy is a composite is often quite difficult because old parts are often used: Take a horse from one toy and a railroad car from another, put them together, and you have a convincing looking complete trolley car. A collector, especially a novice, could be easily fooled.

Buying late nineteenth-century tin toys that have missing parts is especially troublesome. Replacement parts can be cast for iron without too much trouble, but not for tin. Tin toys made after 1930 are much more plentiful than the earlier ones, and so the possibility of finding a replacement part for them is much greater. With the earlier toys, your chances are fairly slim. When considering making a purchase, always look for holes where a missing part may have been located and for parts that have been resoldered. In the case of a resoldered toy, if the job is neatly done and original parts are used to replace those missing, the value of the toy will not drop substantially. Repainted parts, on the other hand, will reduce a toy's worth considerably.

The ideal situation, of course, would be for a collector to know every toy ever made by every manufacturer in every color combination, but this much information could probably never be assembled by any one person. What is more practical for a collector is to be able to recognize certain toy types and

The Hero (late 1880s–1890s). Of all collectible toys, trains constitute the largest group, and many collectors find the earlier ones the most attractive of all. This early group (pre–1900) consists of many trains that were not powered by a motor of any sort. These are referred to as floor trains, and a very fine example is the train pictured here. The Hero is constructed of tin except for the wheels and axles, which are of cast iron. The engine is predominantly black, with red trim and gold stenciling. The tender is also black with gold trim, while the box cars are painted red with gold stenciling. Though the engine and tender appear to have had some restoration work done to them, the toy is still a most desirable piece. The cars are original. As regards the manufacturer, this train, which is nearly 3 feet long, has been attributed to the James Fallows Company of Philadelphia, Pennsylvania. RICHARD MERRILL.

note that subtle differences do occur. In the horses, for example, note the tails, the gait, the way in which the saddle is stenciled, the smoothness or roughness of the mane, the style of the wheels (if there are any) that the horse is standing upon, and the other stylistic differences that may differentiate one manufacturer from another. Then do some more research and ask questions.

A few manufacturers imprinted their toys with a trademark. For example, Hull & Stafford, Ives (sometimes), and Francis, Field & Francis occasionally marked their toys, especially their later ones. But most companies did not, as a courtesy to their jobbers or salesmen who sometimes sold toys from more than one company. To keep the retailers from dealing directly with the manufacturers, thus cutting jobbers out of the picture, jobbers sometimes requested that no trade names be used on the wares. And since jobbers sold the majority of the toys produced, manufacturers usually agreed to this request. The jobbers, then, are the ones to blame for our difficulty in assigning manufacturers' names to pieces.

As far as value is concerned, the larger tin toys tend to bring better prices at auction than the smaller ones. They were more costly to make and sell, so fewer were manufactured. Surprisingly, as noted, tin was a somewhat over-looked field until recently, but now it seems to be the only game in town; this is especially true of the early American and German hand-painted examples.

The later tin toys are also finding a larger following than ever before. From the early 1900s until 1930, millions of fabulous tin toys were produced all around the world. Into the 1950s, except during the war years when tin was replaced by wood, this metal is what most toys were made from. Tin was easy to work with, took to lithography or paint very well, and was inexpensive. As a result, millions of great toys were introduced to the world market every year. Then came plastic, but we will leave that for another book.

Naturally, tin toys made after 1930 are more plentiful than the earlier ones, and as an added bonus, they can sometimes be found in their original boxes. They are almost always marked, and because they are well documented, they are easy to research.

The tin toys for which most established collectors will be on the lookout are the older ones that were produced by such companies as Strauss, Bing, Maerklin (all German manufacturers), Hafner, Ives, Lehmann, Brown, Bergmann, Stevens, Lindstrom, Wilkins, and Nifty (most noted for its comic-strip toys). Marx is another name to be reckoned with in the future, as can be seen even now according to auction results. And don't forget the Japanese toys; but we will talk more about them in a later chapter.

A number of excellent books have been written over the past few years with the tin-toy collector in mind. Quite a few of them will be mentioned later in our bibliography. For serious collectors, having as many resource books at their fingertips as possible is of the utmost importance. For the novice, resource books are doubly important.

CAST-IRON TOYS

Cast-iron toys have lost some of their appeal, and except for the larger or rarer pieces, cast iron has definitely "softened" in value. This trend is a direct result of reproductions, many of which are old and excellent copies. The collector should not fear, however, because these trends are cyclical, and cast iron will come into its own again.

During the 1870s, when tin toys were at the peak of their popularity, toy manufacturers began to explore the possibilities of cast iron. Tin, they reasoned, was just not durable enough, and more importantly, cast iron could be produced more cheaply. Cast iron was much more durable and had been used successfully before 1870 to make some banks, cannons, and cap pistols. One by one, manufacturers began to experiment, and within ten years, toy manufacture underwent a transition that would produce some of the finest toys ever seen.

During the 1880s and 1890s, whole toy lines were developed, especially

A top-of-the-line, Ives No. 1-gauge 3240 electric cast-iron locomotive. The engine pictured here is the first in Ives's 3240 series and dates to 1912. C. L. COLLINS.

horse-drawn vehicles, banks, and trains (one of the largest areas of collecting interest right from the start). Whole new vistas began to open up for toy manufacturers as the use of cast iron became a virtual art form. Creative genius took sway as new and elaborate toys were created. One cannot help but marvel at the engineering and artistic beauty of the many mechanical banks and the almost inexhaustible number of fire engines, circus wagons, brakes (wagons), hansom carriages, and trains that just poured from the foundries in what seemed like a never-ending stream.

Among the older cast-iron toy manufacturers, Ives and Carpenter are two giants. Their toys have been valued by collectors ever since the earliest days of the hobby.

Francis Carpenter began to produce toys in New York during the 1880s and 1890s, and his toys have become one of the most sought-after groups. Their beauty, style, and quality are rivaled only by Ives toys. (Sometimes the toys of the two companies are confused for each other.) Carpenter is especially noted for trains and fire-fighting toys, but most coveted by collectors is Carpenter's Burning Building. This toy consists of the façade of a building that is on fire, an occupant of the building, and two ladders with firemen on them. When a lever is pulled, the firemen climb the ladders and rescue the occupant, a very Victorian-looking lady, who is stranded on the second-floor balcony.

The Cutter Sleigh (ca. 1890s). Finding two toys that are similar in nature and can be used as comparison pieces, as in the case here, is always interesting. Ascertaining who manufactured them, and when, is not always easy. Both toys pictured appear to have been manufactured by the same company, even though there are stylistic differences in the sleighs, the figures, and, of course, the animals. Both toys appeared on the market as early as the 1890s. We find them again being advertised about 1903, and the reindeer-drawn toy appears again in the 1920s. We believe that both were manufactured by the Hubley Company of Lancaster, Pennsylvania. Top: This horse-drawn toy is all cast iron and is about 15 inches long. The horse is white with black trim (it is interesting to note that there is only one animal; this toy sometimes came with two). The sleigh is dark green with gold trim on the sides and back. The rider is a brunette dressed in a pink outfit. Bottom: This reindeer-drawn toy is also all cast iron and is about 16½ inches long. The reindeer are brown and the front wheels are red. The sleigh is dark green with gold trim only on the sides. The figure is a different casting than that in the horse-drawn sleigh. Her outfit is a purple shade, and she is a blonde. Other figures were also employed with this toy, including Santa Claus, the woman pictured, a man with a moustache, and a comic character. The sleigh was also produced in a smaller size with one reindeer, and white reindeer were used on still another variation. RICHARD MERRILL.

Toys by Carpenter, especially the horse-drawn pieces, are fairly easy to identify. The horse-drawn toys usually have a toothed wheel located under the horse. This wheel, which is connected to wires attached to the horse, catches in the rug when the toy is pushed and causes the horse to "gallop" up and down. Patent dates of November 1870 or March 1883 were often embossed on the shaft between the horses.

The Ives toys are a bit harder to identify because few were marked prior to 1905, but many collectors claim to be able to recognize them just by the quality and beauty of the casting. What is undeniable is their desirability. Probably no other toy company creates quite as much of a stir in a collector.

A contemporary of Carpenter and Ives was the Pratt and Letchworth Company of Buffalo, New York. Although most noted for horse-drawn fire-fighting equipment, this company also manufactured large cast-iron floor trains. (Floor trains are pulled and do not have flanged wheels, a power source, or a track.) Still another producer of cast-iron toys at that time was the Wilkins Company of Keene, New Hampshire. Wilkins manufactured numerous horse-drawn vehicles, including a water tower and a fire-fighting wagon that are over a foot long.

In the early part of the 1900s, Wilkins was absorbed into the Kingsbury Manufacturing Company. Toys produced by Kingsbury are noted for their rubber tires stamped "Kingsbury," and most are propelled by a rather large, distinguishable clockwork mechanism located underneath the toy.

Two other notable producers of cast-iron toys were the Hubley Manufacturing Company of Lancaster, Pennsylvania, and the Kenton Hardware Company of Kenton, Ohio. Both companies have long histories of toy production, from the early 1900s through the 1940s and 1950s. They are known for the quality and inventiveness of the horse-drawn toys, fire engines, planes, blimps, comic-strip toys (many of which are extremely rare today), and banks that poured from their factories. Of special note are the Hubley Four-Seated Brake (circa 1910), which has an overall length of almost thirty inches; the Kenton comic-strip toys, such as the Sight-Seeing Bus (1911), which carries the figures of Mama Katzenjammer, Happy Hooligan, Alfonse and Gaston, and the Captain; and Happy Hooligan's Police Patrol (Kenton—circa 1929) in which Hooligan is hit over the head by a police officer as the toy is pulled along.

During the 1920s, Hubley introduced the extremely popular Royal Circus series. As a set, it is somewhat rare today. Even though this series has appeared to have "softened" in price a bit over the past year, it is still a desirable and quite expensive addition to a collection. Circus toys have always been a popular group, and the series by Hubley has everything going for it. The set includes, among others things, a Band Wagon (about sixteen or eighteen inches long), pulled by four horses and manned by eight musicians and a

The City of New York *(ca. 1903). This is a great toy and is somewhat difficult to find, especially in good condition.* The City of New York *was one of the fleet of cast-iron paddleboats manufactured by the Harris Company. Two of the other members of the fleet included a much smaller version of the boat pictured (no name was painted on it) and an intermediate-size boat named the* Puritan. *Made of cast iron, the* City of New York *is an impressive toy measuring nearly 16 inches long. It is painted white with red trim. The two rear paddle wheels are painted red, the name is blue, and the smokestack is black. Both floor toys, the* City of New York *and the* Puritan *had offset front wheels that caused the ships to bob up and down when pulled. A realistic-looking toy, the one pictured is also in excellent original condition, which adds to its historical importance. The Dent Company also manufactured similar cast-iron paddleboats, but they were not as detailed or charming as those by Harris.* RICHARD MERRILL.

driver; a Revolving Animal-Cage Wagon (as the wagon is pulled along the animals inside revolve); and a Giraffe Wagon.

Kenton also came out with a circus series known as the Overland Circus. This set appeared during the 1940s and continued to be popular into the early 1950s. An easy-to-find three-piece set, the Overland Circus consists of a Polar-Bear Cage Wagon, pulled by two horses with riders; a Calliope Wagon; and a Band Wagon, with six musicians. Although certainly not old, the Overland Circus is charming and a fun toy to own. And quite often, the three pieces can be found in near-mint condition.

The Arcade Manufacturing Company of Freeport, Illinois, is another toy manufacturer of considerable importance. Cast iron seems to have been its favorite medium as it turned out toys of every description during the 1920s, 1930s, and 1940s. Most of its cars and trucks are marked with an embossed "Arcade." Some of them also have a paper label affixed to the door. One of this company's most popular automotive toys was the Yellow Cab, which was modeled after cabs of the late 1920s, having a square roof and all. A great toy, not especially hard to find, and still affordable, the Yellow Cab was manufactured by a few different companies, but Arcade seems to have been the only one that marked the toy.

Other cast-iron toys include bell toys, in which a bell rings when the toy is pulled or pushed along the floor. Many are simple—the bell actually rings itself when the clappers swing. Others are more complex—the movement of figures rings the bell. Many of the more complex bell toys rival mechanical banks for their ingenuity and charm, and all seem to be highly desirable to collectors.

A few of the companies that manufactured bell toys were J. E. Stevens of

A calliope wagon from the Overland Circus (ca. 1948). During the early 1940s and into the early 1950s, the Kenton Hardware Company manufactured a group of three circus wagons, including the one pictured. Included were the calliope wagon, a bandwagon, and a cage wagon (with a polar bear). All three wagons are cast iron, brightly colored in red, yellow, and silver, and make a great addition to any toy collection. Not as old or as rare as the Royal Circus wagons by Hubley (ca. 1920s), the Overland Circus wagons are still every bit as charming as their precursors.
RICHARD MERRILL.

A Surrey with a Fringe on Top (1951). When the stage play Oklahoma *was so popular, the Stanley Toy Company introduced its own version of a Surrey with a Fringe on Top. Made of cast aluminum and pot metal, the Surrey is an easy toy to find but one that has great growth potential. The castings are excellent, and the toy can often be found in its original box. The Stanley Company did not intend its Surrey to be a reproduction of an earlier toy. The Surrey was original in nature and, as such, has value as a collectible toy.* C. L. COLLINS.

Cromwell, Connecticut; the N. N. Hill Company of East Hampstead, Connecticut; the Waltrous Company of East Hampton, Connecticut (later absorbed into the N. N. Hill Company); and the Gong Bell Company, one of the world's largest suppliers of bells, also of East Hampton. Stevens also produced mechanical banks (for which the company is most noted), still banks and safes, cap pistols, toy cannons, and numerous parts for other companies. The company was founded in the 1840s and had been in business for over one hundred years when finally forced to close its doors.

Cast-iron toys were so popular that production of them continued until the outbreak of World War II, when cast iron was needed for other reasons. The fact that the metal was used in the production of toys up to this date presents some problems to new collectors, who may think that a cast-iron piece is older than it actually is. With a little research, however, one can usually date a toy. Price does not necessarily correlate with age; some of the more desirable cast-iron toys were made between 1910 and 1930.

After the war, cast-iron toys saw some short-lived popularity. One toy produced in the 1950s that was not a reproduction of an earlier toy was the Surrey with a Fringe on Top. It was made by the Stanley Company in an effort to capitalize on the popularity of the musical *Oklahoma*. A similar toy made by Kenton is a bit harder to find, and, although the Stanley toy is less than thirty years old, it has become a collectible, especially among newer collectors.

Space does not allow a listing of all the toy companies engaged at one time or another in the production of cast-iron toys; but their omission here does not in any way lessen their importance in the field.

CHAPTER 5

Steam Toys and Trains

STEAM TOYS

An extremely fascinating group of toys are the steam toys, toys which might be described as of double interest because they not only reproduce real objects in appearance and motion, but actually work in exactly the same manner as do their proto-types. Just as in the full-sized ones, the toys present a boiler to be filled with water, a fire to be fueled and lighted and a head of steam raised, and, finally, a resulting symphony of motion that never fails to thrill.*

Toys that use steam as their motive power have always attracted a large following among young and old alike. Even before their widespread manufacture, steam toys were thought to be quite extraordinary and graced the scientific cabinets of many a prestigious university. They were something of an intellectual curiosity that tended to baffle and amuse both students and professors.

Steam toys first appeared in the 1860s, but there does not seem to have been any serious manufacture of them in the United States until the 1870s. At this time the Buckman Manufacturing Company of Brooklyn, New York, started producing steam toys in appreciable quantities. This company was most noted for the Young America steam engine, which was offered as a premium by the newspaper *Youth's Companion*. This small engine stood upright

* Louis Hertz, *The Handbook of Old American Toys* (Weathersfield, Conn.: Mark Haber & Co., 1974), p. 42.

on three legs and had a small alcohol burner that slipped underneath. "A driving wheel for machinery is attached to every engine" was one of the company's boasts about this toy. This well-designed engine is somewhat rare today and is quite desirable.

In 1871 the Eugene Beggs Company of Patterson, New Jersey, produced live-steam trains that ran on a fixed radius of wooden track. A strip of metal was embedded in either rim to prevent the train from running off the track, a common design before trains were equipped with flanged wheels that ran on the rails themselves.

Some firms also produced live-steam fire engines, boats, and road-working equipment. The Weeden Company of New Bedford, Massachusetts, was one of these firms. In fact, Weeden was one of the most long-lived of all producers of live-steam toys.

In 1885, Weeden began selling a nine-inch-long steamboat that consisted of a hull, a boiler, and a smokestack. The flame was provided by a small brass lamp that slid under the boiler. With the boiler fired up, and a piece of string attached so as not to lose the toy, this small boat could battle the dangers of many a pond for more than fifteen minutes at a time.

Fourteen years later, Weeden manufactured and marketed the Dart, one of the most successful steam trains ever produced in the United States. This

Right: *A No. 1 Weeden Upright steam engine (1880s). During the 1880s the Weeden Company introduced its first horizontal steam engine, only one in a line that would make Weeden the name in steam toys. The steam engine pictured stands approximately 10 inches tall, is made of pressed tin and cast iron, and came equipped with a steam gauge and shut-off valve. A small alcohol burner fit under the base of the engine.* Left: *The accessory is of German manufacture, is hand-painted tin, and works by means of a pulley wheel (ca. 1912). The little man futilely attempts to saw through a tin log.* C. L. COLLINS.

*An interesting blend of the old and the new. The postwar Maerklin HO locomotives
are pictured with a number of early Ives O-gauge engines, cars, and stations.*
C. L. COLLINS.

*The famous Weeden Dart live-steam locomotive with accompanying tender and box
car (ca. 1888). This set is unusual in that it has an eight-wheel tender; the majority
have only four.* RICHARD MERRILL.

train consisted of an engine, a tender, and one lightweight boxcar. The track was wooden with metal strips and was similar to the earlier track by Beggs. Dart sets all bear the date 1888, even though this train was made in vast quantities up to 1910. Locating one in really good condition is difficult. The Dart originally sold for $3.50 but tends to bring a bit more than that now from train enthusiasts.

Some companies also produced accessories that were powered by stationary steam engines. Every conceivable type of miniature machine was manufactured. By means of pulleys and interlocking gears, steam engines ran lathes, sharpened knives, rocked cardboard babies, cut wood, and ran miniature machine shops all over the United States.

Operating instructions for the Weeden Dart (ca. 1888). This set of instructions came packed with each set of trains and the importance of proper operation was greatly stressed. C. L. COLLINS.

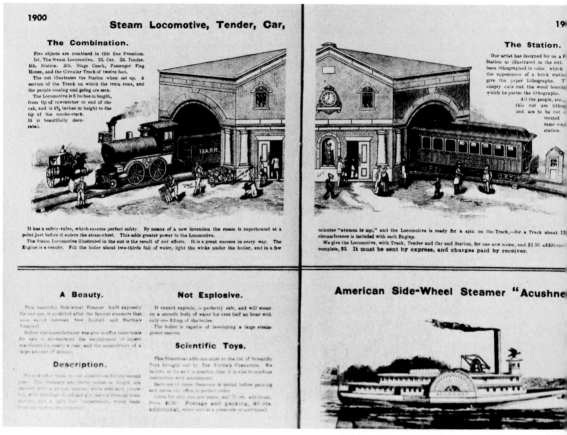

This advertisement was taken from The Youth's Companion *magazine (1880s), which offered the train and a wooden, paper-lithographed station as a subscription premium.* RICHARD MERRILL.

These early steam accessories usually were made either of colorfully lithographed cardboard or of tin. The tin accessories were hand painted, lithographed, or both. Many of these accessories were made in the United States, but many more were imported from Europe, especially from Germany. Regardless of their place of manufacture, these early accessories are eagerly sought out by collectors of live-steam, tin, and cardboard toys.

The age of a steam engine is fairly easy to ascertain. If it stands on three legs and is somewhat squat, it is one of the earlier ones. If it has more than three legs or no legs at all, it belongs to the intermediate period (1880–1920). If it has an indentation to accept an electrical plug, it is one of the newer ones. While the electrics are collectible in their own right, the older engines are the ones most in demand. Electric steam engines were being produced into the 1950s, and some are still being produced today. Some alcohol-fired toys are being manufactured today because of the interest in antique toys, but the most widely collected group were produced no later than 1910.

A word of caution about old live-steam toys: They are attractive to display, but no matter how complete one may appear to be, do not to try to fire it up. At the very best, the toy will probably be damaged, and at worst, it could give way and perhaps explode. Remember, fittings and gauges that are at least fifty years old should not be expected to work. However, placing crushed dry ice into the boiler should generate enough steam to operate the toy without danger of damage to the toy or the operator.

TRAINS

Toy trains have had an allure all their own since the earliest days of their production. During the last three decades of the nineteenth century, children longed to own beautiful tin locomotives that would, when wound, go scurrying off along imaginary tracks laid across the parlor floor. Glorious names such as Meteor, Hercules, Lafayette, Grant, Lightning, Tiger, and Grand Duke adorned many of these early tin toys.

In addition to the trackless "push" and clockwork train sets, there were also available many European-manufactured locomotives that were driven by live steam. Tiny alcohol burners provided the heat necessary to convert the water in the locomotive's boiler to steam. Children found these toys irresistible because they often looked authentic and were propelled like an actual working train.

As time went on, the live-steam train lost much of its popularity because parents feared that the use of alcohol and the open flames would hurt their youngsters. However, cast iron allowed the toy manufacturers of the 1880s to fill the gap left by the disappearance of the live steamers. Although some early cast-iron trackless locomotives were equipped with powerful clockwork mechanisms, most were pull toys that ranged in size from tiny engines with connecting tenders to large, elaborate, and finely constructed models.

Cast-iron locomotives and their accompanying rolling stock proved to be very popular and continued in production well into the twentieth century. Cast-iron trains competed at this time with wooden ones, which were constructed by pasting colorful lithographed paper onto a wooden frame. Some notable producers of wooden toy trains were Crandall, Bliss, Milton Bradley, and Reed.

During the 1880s and 1890s no American-made tracked trains were available, and large mail-order firms imported and distributed many cheaply constructed, lightweight train sets. The firms of Issamayer and Bub made trains entirely of embossed or lithographed tin, with clockwork mechanisms that contained little brass or iron.

As early as 1850, electricity was used as a means of propulsion, much to

the delight of early train enthusiasts. In 1896 the Carlisle and Finch Company of Cincinnati, Ohio, actively manufactured 2-inch-gauge electric trolley cars. The line soon consisted of beautifully embossed brass, four- and eight-wheeled trolleys and a coal-mining train. Electric streetcars were also being manufactured in Germany at this time by Georges Carette and Co. of Nuremberg. However, electricity was "newfangled," and electric trains were considered to be merely a curiosity or a piece of scientific apparatus. Clockwork-powered trains were to dominate the market for several years to come.

The year 1900 found one Joshua Lionel Cowen busily at work in New York producing a number of large 2⅞-inch-gauge streetcar models. This early line included a model of the Baltimore & Ohio Railroad tunnel locomotive, an open as well as a closed trolley, a motorized gondola, a motorized derrick, and a motorized express car. The bodies for the open trolleys were purchased from the Morton Converse Company of Winchendon, Massachusetts. The Converse was manufactured as either a trackless pull toy or as a trackless clockwork model.

In 1906, Lionel abandoned the 2⅞-inch-gauge models and introduced the first standard-gauge model, which included the first inside third-rail sectional tin-plate track ever produced in this country. In 1915, Lionel began its O-gauge line but continued production of standard-gauge models until the early 1940s.

Early Carlisle and Finch electric toy-railroad equipment (late 1880s). The mining locomotive and coal cars, as well as the four-windowed electric railway trolley, are constructed with embossed brass bodies, wooden frames, and cast-iron wheels. RICHARD MERRILL.

The Voltamp Electric Manufacturing Company of Baltimore was begun in 1903 by Manes E. Fuld. This firm produced many beautiful 2-inch-gauge electric trains. In 1923, however, Voltamp sold its line of toy trains to the H.E. Boucher Manufacturing Company of New York. Boucher is best known for its realistic version of the Blue Comet, a crack passenger train that regularly ran between New York and New Jersey. Boucher passed from the toy-train manufacturing scene in 1934.

David W. Knapp founded the Knapp Electric & Novelty Company of New York in 1890. Knapp originally manufactured a line of motors, fans, "shockers," (hand-cranked generators that created a shock to startle the recipiant) and the very popular Knapp Electric Questionnaire. Knapp began its short-lived venture into electric toy-train manufacturing in 1904, producing large, well-proportioned 2-inch-gauge cast-iron engines and a line of paper-covered tin freight and passenger cars. Knapp was the only manufacturer to produce a large 2-inch-gauge *cast-iron* locomotive.

The 1900s witnessed the birth of yet another short-lived toy-train manufacturer, the Howard Miniature Lamp Company of New York. The Howard

An early Knapp Company electric train set lettered for the New York Central and Hudson River Railroad (1904). RICHARD MERRILL.

An early Maerklin O-gauge clockwork locomotive (ca. 1898–1900). RICHARD MERRILL.

line was created around 1905 and included a novel, dual-purpose electric car —a motorized gondola over which fitted a trolley body. The youngster who could not choose between a freight car or a passenger car was doubly satisfied upon receiving a Howard product. Although this company survived as a toy-train manufacturer only until 1919, it is famous in toy-train history for manu-facturing the first locomotive with a working headlight.

At this time, such European firms as Maerklin, Bing, Basset-Lowke, and Hornby were also manufacturing fine models, many of which were similar in design to the American trains and made in hopes of competing in the United States. These European trains have become highly desirable and are keenly sought by collectors.

Upon first discussing the subject of trains with a collector, one immedi-ately becomes aware of a strange language, a tongue that blends ordinary Eng-lish with an infusion of numerical phrases. Numbers such as 25, 40, 42, 381, 1694, 1911, 3243, and 3245 are only a few of the more common sounds in the train collector's vocabulary. In addition, such phrases as "O-gauge," "standard gauge," "No. 1 gauge," and an occasional "No. 2 gauge" or "2⅞ gauge" can often be detected in a train collector's vocabulary. Though their dialects may vary tremendously, all train collectors have an impressive com-mand of this highly specialized language.

The beginning collector will soon realize that numbers are of vital impor-tance. When speaking of gauge, the collector is simply referring to the distance from the inside edge of one running rail to the inside edge of the other running

A hand-painted Maerklin turnstyle (ca. 1910). C. L. COLLINS.

rail. The most common gauges are HO (¾ inch, or 16.5mm), S (⅞ inch, or 22.25mm), O (1¼ inch, or 32mm), No. 1 (1¾ inch, or 45mm), No. 2 (2 inch or 51mm), and 027 (the same width as O-gauge track but lighter), used by Lionel, replaced the Lionel Jr. Line.

The numbers assigned to various models by the different manufacturers allow the collector to specify a particular model immediately. However, when

Two early Maerklin hand-painted station signals (1900). C. L. COLLINS.

A Lionel standard-gauge No. 402 twin-motor engine (1925), pictured with 418-series passenger cars and the original box for the set. RICHARD MERRILL.

collectors discuss a certain model, more than just the model number is often needed. Manufacturers often retained the same number on a locomotive even though the particular model changed radically over a period of years. Many manufacturers also placed the same number on completely different pieces of equipment and even gave the same number to all the pieces in a complete line. Many of the early locomotives may have no number at all, making identification impossible unless the collector has taken the time and effort to study the large variety of trains produced in this country during the first two decades of the twentieth century.

Where can interested beginners go to acquaint themselves with the fascinating yet sometimes baffling pieces of train equipment? Visits to museums, auctions, and large flea markets can prove extremely beneficial. Also, there are many organizations devoted solely to the hobby of collecting model trains. No matter what your taste in trains may be, there is probably another established collector nearby who will be more than happy to help you get started in the hobby and will be delighted to answer all your specific questions. Train collectors are a congenial lot as a whole and are always ready to welcome a fellow enthusiast into their ranks.

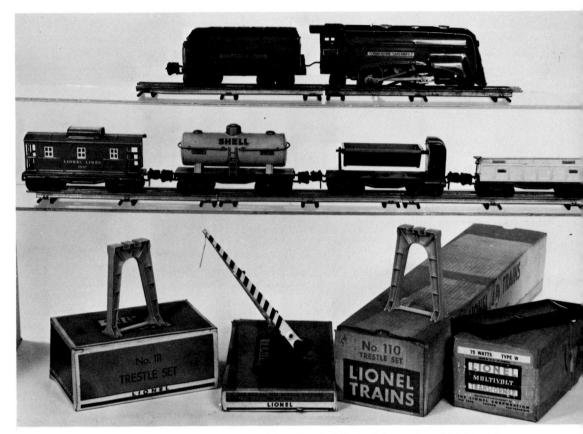

A Lionel No. 265E Commodore Vanderbilt freight set (ca. 1935) with accompanying accessories. RICHARD MERRILL.

The popular streamlined Lionel O-gauge Flying Yankee *(1935–1941).* RICHARD MERRILL.

Many train collectors choose to display older models behind glass, which both enhances the intrinsic beauty of the collection and protects it from dust and moisture. Shared by many collectors is the goal of the nation's first organization devoted to the hobby, the Train Collector's Association (TCA)—to protect the remaining examples of tin-plate trains from the ravages of time. Very few other toys have mirrored the development of this country as toy trains have, beginning with the crude steam models of the 1870s and developing in form and beauty almost as rapidly as their real railroad counterparts did. Streetcars, wood-burning and coal-burning locomotives, and the early electric engines seen so frequently on American railroads have now all but vanished. However, their spirit and form have been preserved in miniature by the men and women who are proud to call themselves train collectors.

Lesser-Known Train Collectibles

Today more information is available to train collectors than at any other time in the history of the hobby. Many fine books and price guides clearly describe, picture, and price the entire toy-train lines produced by major manufacturers. Such books describe even minute variations among the engines, rolling stock, and accessories and have been a tremendous aid to Lionel, American Flyer, and Marx collectors. In addition, European train enthusiasts have recently been barraged with many volumes written on Bing, Maerklin, Carrette, and Fleishman, to name just a few.

We can probably state fairly that most, if not all, collectors have at least one of the now-famous and, we might add, quite collectible articles and books by Louis Hertz. Surprisingly, with the exception of Mr. Hertz's books, little has been written and pictured about collecting Ives trains and the American models that competed with Ives in the early part of the twentieth century. Most modern publications barely touch on this most interesting area. We hope that the following material will serve to guide those collectors interested in the early products of the Ives Corporation and its later competitors.

The Ives Manufacturing Corporation: Perhaps the major problem facing the new collector is one of identification. Most Ives products made in the period from 1901 to 1907 bear absolutely no markings by which the collector can identify the pieces. Early locomotives are also devoid of markings and bear only a painted red stripe below the cab's windows; and the cars are usually hand painted. How, then, can the aspiring Ives collector positively identify these early models?

Perhaps the best way to become familiar with these early pieces of equipment is to visit a collector who is knowledgeable in this field. Most collectors do not specialize in collecting Ives, yet many have several fine examples in their collections and are delighted to share their knowledge with the novice.

An Ives inboard-truck O-gauge baggage car (1904–1905). Note the famous road-name, Limited Vestibule Express. C. L. COLLINS.

There is no better method of learning about these models than to actually see and, more importantly, handle them.

Early Ives catalogs are a source of identifying information. Engines, cars, and accessories are accurately pictured, often in true colors. Although these catalogs are exceedingly scarce, many fine reprints are offered for sale.

Prior to 1904, most of Ives's rolling stock was hand painted and bore no identifying marks. However, in 1904, Ives began to apply the process of lithography to its toy-train cars and accessories. Although the toys did not actually bear a mark that stated they were specifically part of the Ives line, most pieces of rolling stock bore the name Limited Vestibule Express. This name was to become one of the most illustrious ever awarded to a toy train and was carried by Ives on its O-gauge passenger series until 1915, when it was replaced by The Ives Railway Lines. The only exceptions are the No. 50, No. 51, and No. 52 five-inch passenger cars first manufactured in 1910. These yellow cars, labeled Pennsylvania Lines, included a baggage car and two pullmans named Newark and Washington. Although Maerklin used the name Limited Vestibule Express on a series of O- and No. 1-gauge cars around 1910, and the American Miniature Railroad Company used it briefly, no other tin-plate manufacturer applied this name to a line, thus making identification of a true Ives piece easier for today's collector.

The No. 1-gauge line of Ives passenger cars first appeared in 1904. These beautifully lithographed yellow and red cars bore the roadname Twentieth Century Limited Express. In addition to a No. 70 mail car, Ives also produced a No. 71 baggage car, the Saint Louis, and a No. 72 pullman, the San Francisco.

In 1910, the roadname was changed to New York Central Lines or Twentieth Century Limited. The No. 71 car became a buffet car and the No. 72 was renamed Chicago. These cars were usually decorated by a wood-grained, white lithography. The last series of No. 1-gauge passenger cars lettered The Ives Railway Lines (the No. 181, No. 182, and No. 183), c. 1915, were painted green.

The early Ives line of freight cars can also present an identification problem to the new collector. The O-gauge freights are devoid of any marking pertaining to manufacturer. Fortunately, Ives devised one of the easiest and most consistent numbering systems for its cars, and numbers are the international language of the train collector. If the novice takes the time to learn the Ives system, identification can be a simple matter.

The earliest freight was the gondola (circa 1902), which was hand painted with horizontal stripping. In 1904, this gondola was lithographed with blue, red and tan vertical stripes. However, no number appeared on the car then. Around 1906, Ives issued a small, lithographed, numbered freight set that determined the pattern for future sets. Included were a No. 53 merchandise car, a No. 55 stock car and a No. 57 caboose. These early pieces had lithographed frames identical to those in the passenger series. However, the merchandise car and the caboose bore the name Fast Freight Line, which was applied to the earliest Ives freights.

At this time, Ives was also producing a larger, four-wheeled, No. 60 series of freights. The cars in this series also had lithographed frames and included a No. 63 gondola, a No. 64 Fast Freight general merchandise car, a No. 65 stock car, and, oddly, a No. 126 caboose. All were equipped with working hand brakes and lithographed, striped roofs, which also aid the collector in the identification process.

A series of early eight-wheeled freights were also born in 1904. These nine-inch cars had no external frame for the wheels and, like their companion passenger cars, are known as "inboard trucks." This set included a No. 125

An Ives No. 125 inboard-truck general merchandise car (1904–1908). Ives used the logo Fast Freight on many of its earliest freight cars. Note the striped, lithographed roof, another Ives trademark. C. L. COLLINS.

Fast Freight general merchandise car, a No. 127 live stock transportation car, a No. 128 gondola car, and a No. 126 Fast Freight caboose. Ives never produced an early eight-wheeled caboose.

While the style of its cars, trucks, and couplers changed over the next few decades, Ives maintained its numbering system as well as its general merchandise and live stock transportation names. These cars are easily recognizable for most bear the Ives name.

Identifying an early Ives engine can pose a problem to the inexperienced collector. The earliest tin engine is painted entirely black and has no markings whatsoever, while the tender, also black, has two red horizontal stripes. The iron engines dating from 1901 to 1906 are painted black with red, silver and gold trim. They, too, have no identifying marks.

Around 1904, Ives applied its initials, I.M.C., to its lithographed tin engine's cab. However, this monogram, standing for the Ives Manufacturing Corporation, was very similar to the Maerklin trademark, and this little Ives engine is often mistaken for a European model. Although Ives continued to produce a tin engine for several more years, it changed the original styling and design considerably. These engines were each assigned a specific number from 0 to 3. To quote the original catalog description, "The only difference in these locos is in finish and a stronger and better movement." Finished in either black or blue lithography, these engines were longer and leaner, having separate sand domes and air tanks, a striped lithographed roof, and a two-windowed cab.

In 1907–1908, Ives dropped its tin-engine line and replaced these small locomotives with a new series made of cast iron. Unable to lithograph the engine's number onto the cab, the company began applying lithographed tin plates to the engines; these plates identified the locomotive as an Ives No. 0, 1, 2, 3, 4, 11, or 17. While Ives had been applying these lithographed number-plates to its No. 1-gauge No. 40 engine since 1904, this was the first use of the plates on its line of O-gauge engines. The company did not, however, use a plate on its deluxe O-gauge engine, No. 25, until 1910.

Note here that, with the exception of the earliest hand-painted models, all other Ives tenders can be easily recognized. The smaller tenders, used with engines 0 to 4, are lithographed in red and black and bear the letters F.E. (Fast Express) No. 1. The medium-sized tenders were used with the early No. 25 and with engines No. 11 and No. 17. These too are finished in red and black litho and bear the name L.V.E. (Limited Vestibule Express) No. 11. The largest O-gauge tender, L.V.E. No. 25, is similarly finished and was used with the No. 25 engine from 1906 to 1910. One-gauge tenders of this period are also finished in red and black but bear the lettering T.C.L.E. No. 40. Used on the No. 40 and later on the No. 41, this marking denotes that this train is the Twentieth Century Limited Express.

When Ives decided to manufacture clockwork-powered trains that ran on

The first Ives O-gauge, No. 17 engine (1902). Note the fancy brass brake and primitive cast-iron wheels. C. L. COLLINS.

A later Ives No. 17 clockwork engine (1906–1908). This engine bears no identifying marks except a red, hand-painted stripe beneath the cab window C. L. COLLINS.

tin-plate tracks, it also committed itself to developing an entire railroad operation for its young customers, and thus The Ives Miniature Railway System was born. Catalogs were issued showing not only the available engines and cars but also an astonishing number of track configurations. In addition, Ives manufactured a wide variety of accessories—freight sheds, waiting platforms, passenger stations, turntables, bumpers, bridges of many styles, automatic crossing gates, semaphores, and track devices designed to automatically stop a train.

As the Ives products became more popular, the accessories became increasingly sophisticated. A turntable with a clockwork motor was provided, a drawbridge that dropped automatically when the train approached was designed, a clockwork-powered swing bridge was developed, realistic scenic background was offered, and passenger stations became more elaborate. Perhaps the crowning achievement in the development of accessories was the creation of the glass-dome station. Beautifully lithographed and named Grand Central Station, this accessory boasted a beautiful leaded-glass shed.

While many early accessories appear to be similar in design, the identification process can be made easier by a thorough study of the manufacturers' catalogs.

True to form, the earliest Ives accessories bear no mention of the manufacturer's name. However, the Ives lithographic design is so distinctive that once a collector learns to recognize it, the identification process becomes a simple matter. Generally red or tan simulated brick lithography is found on the larger Ives buildings, although some are finished in a simulated wood-grain pattern. On the wood-grained buildings and on some of the wood-grained cars, the detail is so good that no two simulated wooden planks are identical! Many of the smaller stations are lithographed in a striped finish; others are painted and have a lithographed door, base, and roof. The predominant lithograph design on the bases of most early Ives accessories is a series of connecting octagons and diamonds. These are found in many colors including red, yellow, tan, blue, and green. Most early doors and roofs are either striped or finished in a diamond pattern.

Ives seemed to delight in frequently changing the color of its lithography on its accessories, as can be best seen in a study of its early bridges. The basic design on the bases and approach ramps is simulated brick, most often tan. But bridges of the same type also come with bases finished in red and black, red and tan, and red and green. The guardrails and girders are also found in an assortment of colors, including red and white, white and blue, and red and tan.

As with its locomotives, Ives attached lithographed plates to many of its early accessories, identifying freight stations, suburban stations, and telegraph and ticket offices. On the larger passenger stations, plates over the doorways read Mens Waiting Room and Ladies Waiting Room. On occasion, an accessory is found bearing a small plate that reads The Ives Miniature Railway System.

Final identifying characteristics are cast-iron door and window inserts and iron chimney tops. These are painted orange, red, or silver and are usually trimmed in gold.

Shortly after 1910, Ives discontinued the use of lithographed nameplates on the accessories and simply included the signs as part of the lithography. In 1911, a new style of building and a more realistic lithographic design were adopted. Doors once designed to slide became fixed, and earlier buildings with open windows and doors were replaced by models with simulated lithographed doors and windows. Many of these windows resemble stained glass, while others picture men and women inside the building. Ives never over-looked detail. When an item was lithographed to appear to be on the outside of a structure, its shadow was lithographed behind it.

The lithographic pattern on the roofs was changed to a series of connect-ing hectagons. The striking reds, greens, and tans of the earlier roofs were abandoned in favor of muted browns and greens. The beautifully colored bridges with their bricklike lithography and intricate steel supports became drab and colorless, usually finished in grays, maroons, and olive greens. Many collectors feel that the Ives accessories after 1910–1911 lost all of their color-ful, toylike charm.

Prior to 1907, most of Ives's competition came from Europe. However, in this year, two new companies emerged as American toy-train manufactur-ers, the American Miniature Railway Company and the Edmonds-Metzel Manufacturing Company.

The American Miniature Railway Company: The fact that the American Miniature Railway Company (AMRR) was founded by two former Ives

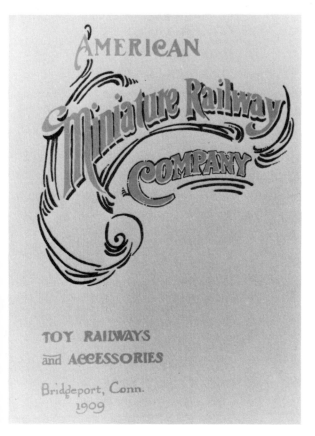

An American Miniature Railway catalog cover (1909). C. L. COLLINS.

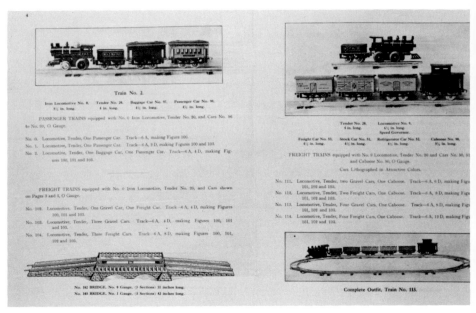

This page from the A.M.R.R. catalog (1909) pictures a small and inexpensive train set. Notice that the passenger car bears the roadname Limited Vestibule Express as well as Chicago, and has a frame identical to those produced by Metzel and Ives. C. L. COLLINS.

This page from the A.M.R.R. catalog (1909) pictures the larger passenger sets. Each car is even equipped with simulated brake shoes. C. L. COLLINS.

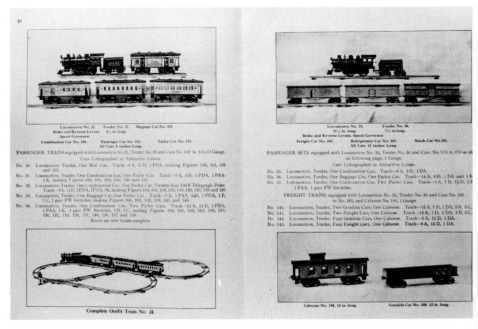

employees can be seen in the striking similarities between the products of both companies. More often than not, when an AMRR engine or car is found, it is mistaken for an Ives. However, very definite differences do exist.

AMRR engines were assigned numbers that were never used by Ives. Its tin engines are extremely similar in design to those manufactured by Ives, yet carry the number 100. Its small iron engine, equivalent to the Ives locomotives Nos. 0–4, is embossed with the number 125 and has a separate tin sand dome. AMRR also produced an engine similar in design to the Ives No. 11, yet this engine is embossed No. 200. Other engines in this series are cataloged as locomotives No. 9 and No. 15. The top-of-the-line O-gauge locomotive resembles the Ives No. 20, except that it is embossed with an unmistakable AMRR. Other cataloged locomotives are assigned the numbers 17, 19, 21 and 35. The No. 1-gauge line includes an engine that is cataloged as No. 41. This engine closely resembles the Ives No. 40, both being constructed with a 4–4–0 wheel arrangement. The AMRR logo is embossed under the cab's window.

AMRR was one of the few companies that used the name Limited Vestibule Express on its cars. Almost identical in size and construction to the smaller Ives cars of this period, the AMRR car is lithographed with the name Chicago, which is commonly associated with the early American Flyer line of toys.

The 1909 AMRR line includes a wide variety of beautifully litographed O-gauge passenger and freight cars. The small 4½-inch cars are all mounted on frames identical to those used by Ives and Edmonds-Metzel. Further evidence of the Ives influence can be seen in the use of tiny vestibules on the passenger cars, a characteristic made famous on the cars of the Ives lines. Close

An American Miniature Railway Company No. 125 clockwork locomotive (1908–1909). This engine is very similar to the small Ives locomotives of the period, except for the cab embossing and the separate tin-sand dome. C. L. COLLINS.

A superb cast-iron clockwork locomotive in No. 1 gauge, manufactured by the American Miniature Railway Company of Bridgeport, Connecticut (1908). Although the American Miniature equipment was well made and attractively finished, the company lasted only five years. The pictured example very closely resembles the Ives No. 40 clockwork locomotive of the same period. The bell is missing on this example. C. L. COLLINS.

examination of the AMRR cars numbered 91, 93, 95, 97, and 98 reveals that they are nearly exact copies of the Ives No. 50 series cars of that period.

The names of the AMRR cars are quite distinctive—Pullman Palace, New York and Boston Express, Empire State Express, and Black Diamond Express. The smaller freight cars are labeled Erie Freight, Live Stock Conveyance, and Merchants Dispatch Transportation Company, while the larger No. 1-gauge freights bear such names as Furniture and Carriage, Santa Fe Refrigerator Line, California Fruit Growers Dispatch, Horse and Cattle, and Eastern Fast Freight Line.

A distinguishing feature employed by AMRR was the use of simulated

An Edmonds-Metzel deluxe locomotive (1907–1908). It has handrails, tin drive rods, and a brake. A green cab stripe, screw key, and fluorescent red wheels help identify this as a Metzel engine. The No. 328 tender has a red frame and body, trimmed in white. C. L. COLLINS.

brake shoes on the 8-inch O-gauge passenger and freight cars and on the 12-inch No. 1-gauge cars.

Despite the wide variety and excellent quality of the items produced by AMRR, the company was somehow unable to compete successfully with the Ives and the new Edmonds-Metzel lines of toy trains and ceased production in 1912.

The Edmonds-Metzel Manufacturing Company "The American Flyer": The Edmonds-Metzel Manufacturing Company's line of tin-plate toy trains first appeared in 1907. W. F. Hafner, in conjunction with the Chicago-based Metzel Hardware firm, supervised the development of an O-gauge line of clockwork trains named "American Flyer" (the name on the car, not the company name). This name became so popular that in 1910, the Edmonds-Metzel Manufacturing Company became the American Flyer Manufacturing Company.

The earliest Metzel "American Flyer" engines have readily recognizable characteristics. Metzel produced only two basic types of locomotive. Although both had an identical cast-iron body, one was a deluxe model, with flat, tin piston rods; iron handrails; and a hand-operated braking mechanism. Typically, Metzel engines are black with green or yellow trim beneath the cab window. The clockwork mechanism is mounted in the iron shell by means of screws, and the wheels are lead with a metallic red finish. These Metzel engines have four narrow, nickle-plated boiler bands and a narrow figure-eight-shaped winding key. The earliest tenders are generally found in a tomato-red finish and have a fixed, hook-slot coupler. They are always numbered 328.

The first Metzel cars, like many other early examples of toy trains, carry no manufacturer's name. The Pullman and Chicago cars have lithographed doors and three lithographed windows. Generally found in handsome blue or red litho, these 4½-inch cars are mounted on frames that appear identical to those of their Ives and AMRR counterparts. Metzel also produced larger, 5-inch cars with cut-out doors and windows. These cars are also labeled Chicago and bear, for the first time, the name American Flyer. These intricately lithographed cars are most often found in beautiful shades of green, blue, or yellow.

Around 1910, American Flyer added another locomotive to its line. This new engine had a snap-in motor, and although it retained the metallic painted-lead wheels, it looked totally unlike its predecessors. The cab was narrowed to produce a streamline effect; the four narrow boiler bands were replaced by two bulky wide ones; and the early, large headlight was reduced in size and placed on the front of the boiler. This engine was the last in the line to have a green stripe under the cab. The cars generally found accompanying this engine are identical in size to the earliest, three-windowed cars of 1907. However, the windows and doors are punched out, rather than lithographed onto the tin sides. Usually found in creamy white, these cars are lettered American Flyer and bear the name Chicago within a blue, red, or green border. This train may be considered a transition set from the Edmonds-Metzel Company to the true American Flyer Company.

Although the early American Flyer Company produced an engine that was very similar in design to the original Metzel engine, American Flyer continued to apply only the wide boiler bands and trimmed beneath the cab in red. Interestingly, most early American Flyer accessories are of obvious European manufacture.

American Flyer began O-gauge electric-train production in 1918 and

An American Flyer, Edmonds-Metzel "transition" locomotive (1910–1913). While this engine retains the Metzel green stripe and fluorescent wheels, the casting has been streamlined, and wide American Flyer boiler bands have been applied. This engine is often found with Edmonds-Metzel passenger cars. Also note that the tender now has a black frame. C. L. COLLINS.

An early American Flyer clockwork locomotive (1914). This engine has Flyer's characteristic red cab stripe, wide boiler bands, and snap-in motor. The tender is black with white lettering. C. L. COLLINS.

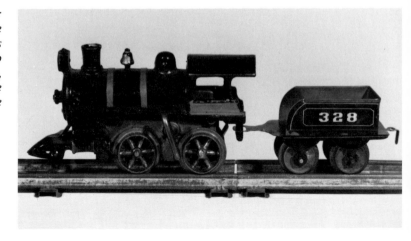

An early American Flyer clockwork freight set (1914–1915). C. L. COLLINS.

standard-gauge electric-train production in 1925. After A. C. Gilbert of New Haven, Connecticut, purchased the firm in 1938, some O-gauge trains were manufactured, but they were soon replaced by the current S-gauge, two-rail track line. In 1914, W. F. Hafner, a producer of toy clockwork automobiles and a friend and former associate of the president of Metzel Hardware, also formed his own line of toy trains, the Hafner Manufacturing Company, which continued production until late in the 1930s.

CHAPTER 6

A Potpourri of Toys

W ithin this chapter, the authors have attempted to introduce the reader to a number of separate and quite diverse groupings of collectible toys. This is not intended to be a definitive work on any particular group. Rather, it is hoped that the information presented here will be helpful to the new collector in the identification and classification processes. For those interested in a further study of one particular catagory of toy, many fine works are currently available which discuss each specific group in great detail. (See bibliography.)

CLOCKWORK TOYS

Wind-up, or clockwork, toys were first produced as an amusement and diversion for the royal heads of Europe. These "automatons," as they are now known, were later adapted for production by American toy makers (at least the same concept was). By the motive power of a clockwork mechanism hidden within the body or base of the toy, lifelike figures became animated and danced, walked, smoked cigars, did somersaults, or drew pictures. Clockwork mechanisms also powered wagons, row boats, tin and cast-iron trains, steamships, and merry-go-rounds. A few even allowed cloth bears to temporarily come to life.

The most important clockwork toys were probably produced in this country between 1865 and 1900. Of these toys, a few basic types can be discerned. The major difference usually rests in the placement of the clockwork itself. One type had the mechanism hidden within the box or podium on which the figure stood. The other type had the clockwork hidden within the figure itself, enabling the figure to walk (for example, Ives manufactured a walking Santa Claus, General Butler, Black Butler, and Chinaman) or perform tricks. Some clockwork toys were even more complicated and could perform more than one task. Ives's General Grant, a seated figure, could turn his head and lift a cigar to his lips. He would appear to puff on the cigar, and smoke, coming from a hidden cigarette and blown by a bellows within the toy, would actually issue from his mouth. Needless to say, this is a rare, prized, and somewhat expensive addition to any collection.

After 1900, American toy manufacturers faced stiff competition from inexpensive European copies and often had to sacrifice quality for low-cost production. Many American firms started to make less expensive clockwork toys of tin to vie with the European influx. Beginning about 1910 and continuing through the 1930s and 1940s, companies like Strauss, Marx, Unique Art, Lindstrom, Wolverine, and Wilkins mass-produced toy lines that competed successfully with their European counterparts, and a whole new era of American toy manufacture was started. High tariffs and more efficient production methods helped the American toy industry to stay alive. However, many purists feel that American toys manufactured after 1930 lack the charm of the earlier toys, are less refined in overall appearance, and are less appealing.

Some of the other important names to look for in the time period of 1900 to 1940 are Lehmann, Carette, Lionel, and Nifty.

From 1940 on one should also look for toys made by Japanese firms like Line-Mar, who were and are prolific manufacturers of many different types of toys. Toys that are battery operated, though not clockwork (technically speaking), fit into this later grouping and, probably within ten years, will be just as popular. Already they are gaining respectability among many collectors from all over the world. This will be one of the groups to watch in the future.

A clockwork, cast-iron floor train probably manufactured by Hubley (ca. 1890s). The classic styling of this little locomotive adds much to its charm. C. L. COLLINS.

BANKS

We are all painfully aware that saving money isn't as easy as it used to be. With inflation, money is getting harder and harder to save, and with the tax on bank interest, the incentive to save has all but disappeared. There was a time, however, when the pace of life was a little slower and when one's money went a lot further. There was a time when saving was not only possible but fun as well.

One wonders, looking back on the history of toy savings banks in this country, whether Ben Franklin could have foreseen the implications of his simple maxim "A penny saved is a penny earned." He extolled worldwide the virtue of saving money and good old Yankee thrift. How many of us, in fact, had it drilled into our heads that thrift and saving were always to be preferred over spending? How many of us had parents that demanded we take a goodly portion of birthday-present money and "Put it away for a rainy day"? And then, no matter how hard it rained, they would never let us see the savings.

Penny banks have existed for centuries. They have been found by archaeologists in Egyptian and Mayan tombs, in China, and throughout Europe. In America, penny banks became popular during the 1700s, when the introduction of hard money (coins) created the need for some place to store it. As could be expected, toy banks were most popular in New England, where they ingrained themselves right into society. Banks became tools used by parents to teach the virtue of thrift and to reward little savers. In fact, throughout the nineteenth and early twentieth centuries, the United States went through an economic boom that was stimulated, at least in part, by the overwhelming compulsion to save. Interestingly, very few patents for mechanical banks were sought or issued after 1929, the year of the stock market crash. An era had ended, and even children's toys were affected.

Toy penny banks are usually classified either by the material used in their production or by their action (or lack of it). The most popular banks are made of pottery, tin, or cast iron. Others are made of wood, glass, and pot metal. And all banks fall into three accepted groupings as far as action is concerned: still, mechanical, and semimechanical.

Pottery Banks

In the early days of bank production, pottery was the most popular medium of which banks were made. After a pottery piece was completed, all that one needed to do was to cut a slot in it and a bank was created; and quite often the bank was the only one of its kind, since it was designed for a specific person. Pottery banks were produced in glazed as well as unglazed finishes, and they were formed to represent, among other things, jugs, animals, people, and houses.

The most notable manufacturer of glazed banks was Bennington Pottery

A grouping of three pottery banks (1870s–1880s). All have some age to them and are finished in a yellow-brown glaze similar to that used by the Bennington Pottery Works during this period. C. L. COLLINS.

in Vermont, which created banks that have a distinctive brownish glaze. Because other firms copied this finish, telling with any certainty whether a bank is definitely Bennington is sometimes difficult. In general, pottery banks are difficult to identify, since most of them were not marked and since they can be made to appear older than they actually are by baking them in an oven for a few days.

When a child wished to retrieve his or her coins, there was usually only one way to do it—with a hammer! Thus, there are relatively few older pottery banks left. For some reason, however, this is one group that is still overlooked by most collectors. And, as such, it could be a good group to start collecting, since the prices are usually reasonable.

Tin Banks

A more accepted but still underrated group is the early tin banks, which were hand painted and stenciled and usually held together by tabs and solder. They were formed into banks, buildings, drums, and numerous other designs and were at the peak of their popularity between 1850 and 1890. Many of the early tin-toy producers, such as Stevens and Stevens and Brown, Bergmann, and others, made banks as part of their inventory; and whenever the maker can be positively identified, the bank's historic (and usually monetary) value increases. These early tin banks, especially the ornate ones, are scarce, since they had to be opened in a similar fashion as the pottery banks, with a hammer and a screwdriver. Very few had removable coin traps.

The use of tin became popular again from 1920 to 1940. During this time a number of fine, and now rare, German tin banks came onto the market; among them were miniatures of a British lion, a bulldog, a teddy bear, an

African native, and (probably the most rare) comedian Harold Lloyd. All of these banks have the same action—the figure's jaw drops to receive the coin. Easier to find, and of lesser value, are the tin banks made by the Chein Company, which produced a number of still banks (globes, baseballs, and so on) and a few mechanical banks. Of the mechanicals, the Monkey and the Elephant are the most common. The Rabbit, which looks a lot like Uncle Wigley, is a little harder to find, and the First National Duck, which portrays Donald Duck in a bank teller's window, is the hardest to find. Of course, this is the most desirable, since it features a Disney character.

Cast-iron Banks

Banks made from cast iron appeared on the scene during the late 1860s and 1870s. They reached their zenith of popularity during the 1880s, when they outnumbered the number of tin and pottery banks combined. Owing to the ease with which the iron could be cast, a seemingly endless variety of banks poured from the foundaries. Accurate portrayals of people, animals, houses, boats, and combinations of these various elements, in both still and

A gathering of owls (1880–1900). From left to right we have the Owl with Book mechanical bank by Kilgore (when a penny is inserted in the book, the owl blinks his eyes); the Be Wise Save Money still bank by A. C. Williams; the Owl on a Square Base still bank and the Owl mechanical bank, both by J. E. Stevens. For the mechanical owl, depressing a lever located in the rear causes the owl to turn its head and deposit a penny. C. L. COLLINS.

mechanical banks, was now possible. An estimated 10,000 still banks and 250 mechanical banks, all different, were produced between 1870 and 1930. Of these, usually the iron are the most popular among collectors.

Most of the cast-iron still banks were poured in two sections and held together with a turnpin or a screw. Some of the older ones were secured with a pin that was rounded over so that the bank could not be opened. This latter group is not very common.

The cast-iron mechanical banks were more complex castings having some moving parts; and many had a coin trap located in the base to open the bank. Banks produced by the Sheppard Hardware Company usually had a square trap that could be opened with a key; banks produced by the J. E. Stevens Company had a round trap that turned to open the bank.

Still Banks

Of still, mechanical, and semimechanical banks, still banks are more numerous, offer the greatest amount of variation, and at the moment are much more affordable. Their relatively low price seems to be only a temporary condition, however, because the still-bank market is becoming more competitive as mechanicals have become harder to obtain. In fact, many mechanical-bank collectors have now reversed their opinion about still banks and are eagerly seeking them out. Fortunately, still banks were manufactured in such large quantities and in so many different styles that building up a fine collection without investing a fortune is still possible. Usually, the exceptionally rare stills are the ones that attract the most advanced collectors, and the more common ones are left to the newer hobbyists.

Determining the maker and date of manufacture of still banks may require a great deal of research, which can be fun as well as frustrating. Still banks, like tin toys, are sometimes hard to trace. Manufacturers seldom put their name on these banks, and the researcher must turn to old manufacturers catalogs for information.

The major manufacturers of still banks were Arcade, A. C. Williams, Hubley, J.E. Stevens, and the Enterprise Manufacturing Company. Subjects include such diverse areas as circus and zoo animals (lions, elephants, seals, monkeys, bears, camels, and buffalos), the little folk (baseball players, football players, cops, firemen, soldiers, sailors, Boy Scouts, mermaids, clowns, sharecroppers, and even Santa Claus), comic-strip characters (Mutt and Jeff, Buster Brown and Tigre, the Campbell Kids, and Andy Gump), airships, automobiles, trolleys, safes, buildings, and national monuments.

Also of great interest are the banks that depict an event or personage, such as Teddy Roosevelt, General Butler, or General Pershing. A John Kennedy bust bank is a contemporary historical figural bank, and it will probably be quite collectible in a few years.

Mechanical Banks

Mechanical, or animated, banks are an extremely popular and yet misunderstood group. A *mechanical bank,* by definition, is one in which some action takes place as a result of a coin's being placed into a receiving slot and an activating lever's being operated (in some cases the weight of the coin activates the mechanism and starts the bank in motion). Whether the coin is actually deposited before, during, or after the action has taken place is unimportant. As long as there is movement, the bank is considered to be a mechanical. The coin is usually deposited within the bank as a result of the action(s) of the figure(s) on the bank.

Cast-iron mechanical banks are the ones to which most collectors turn, but the German and early American tin banks, such as the Alligator in Tin Trough, the Frog and Snake, and the Weeden's Plantation, are also very desirable.

In today's market there is really no such thing as a "common" cast-iron mechanical bank. Those that were made for a number of years, such as the Tammany and the Owl (whose head turns), are easier to find, but even they are becoming more difficult to obtain.

Price is one factor that separates the common from the rare. Some mechanicals that sold for as little as $10 in the 1950s many now sell for $100; still others, the exception rather than the rule, have been known to fetch prices into the thousands.

Action is also of prime interest to many collectors. The Girl in the Victorian Chair, for example, is a rare bank, yet its action is extremely simple. When a coin is dropped into the bank, a lever is activated, causing the small dog seated on the girl's lap to move. Some collectors do not especially like this bank because of its limited action, but because of its rarity, they would like to have an example in their own collections. On the other hand, a popular but more common bank, the Speaking Dog, has a highly complicated action that is both quaint and amusing. A coin is placed on a plate held by a seated girl. When a lever at the dog's foot is pressed, the girl drops the coin into the bench on which she is seated. At the same time, the dog's mouth opens. After the lever has been released, the dog's mouth closes, but his tail wags for a few seconds in anticipation of another coin. Thus a rare bank does not necessarily have a more complex action than a common one.

Most collectors do seem to have one thing in common, however, when buying a bank or any type of old toy: They look for condition. A bank that has been repainted or restored or one that is in poor condition will be much harder to sell than one that is in good original condition. Condition will be elaborated on further in a later chapter.

A word of caution: Mechanical as well as still banks have been heavily reproduced over the past twenty years, and many of these reproductions are quite good. They have been known to fool the experts, and so it is safe to assume that they could fool a novice too.

Semimechanical Banks

This group has been left for last because it seems to attract little attention among the majority of bank collectors. Semimechanicals include cash-register banks and a few stills, like the Elephant, which moves its trunk slightly when a penny is dropped into the slot. The classification "semimechanical" bothers some collectors, who feel that these banks should be included in one of the other two groups. For this reason, this group will probably be absorbed into either the still or full-mechanical category sometime in the future.

TOY CANNONS AND CAP PISTOLS

A number of years ago, miniature cannons, with real gunpowder or salutes, were used by eager young boys to announce the Fourth of July. A celebration without their loud booming was unthinkable. Unfortunately, many of

A grouping of cast-iron cap pistols (1860s–1905). The earliest models have open-work handles, while the later pistols have trigger guards and more closely resemble actual guns. The nickel-finished model on the right is an early water pistol. C. L. COLLINS.

these cannons were of lightweight design and, when fired, would flip over backward, sometimes bruising or even breaking little fingers. Many of the cannons manufactured after 1870 were adapted to fire caps rather than powder, and although less noise was produced, the toys were less dangerous. This type of cannon reached its vogue in the period from 1885 to 1900. During this time the salute cannon was also popular. The salute was inserted into a breach, and a wick was pulled through the opening provided for it. With the touch of a match there came a fairly safe flash and a resounding boom.

From these early cannons, the cap pistol naturally and concurrently developed. Keeping weapons and even carrying them was still a commonplace practice at the turn of the century, and so naturally young boys would want to emulate the adult males' interest in firearms. Concerned parents realized, however, that the handling of a real gun was too much responsibility for many young children, and so a market was created for toy pistols and rifles. This trend culminated in the eventual development and manufacture of air, BB, and other pellet guns. However, these guns are not included in our discussion because most of them did not fire caps and so form a subgroup of their own. Those manufactured before 1920 are difficult to find, and those manufactured after 1920 do not appear to have had a very large following. Also, in many states these guns are treated as real weapons rather than toys. This fact detracts from their appeal among the majority of toy collectors.

Cap pistols, however, are popular and they can be found dating back to the late 1860s or early 1870s. These early guns are easily recognized by their simple construction. Many of them have openwork handles or no real handle at all. Others have a hammer rather than a defined trigger. They served the purpose, but their resemblance to actual pistols ends there.

The later pistols, those made in the 1880s and 1890s, are more like today's models. Colorful names like Pluck, Cowboy, Crack, Hero, and Challenge were embossed into their sides to entice young gun slingers. Many of these pistols were manufactured by the Ives Company (most noted for its trains and clockwork toys), the Hubley Company, and the J. E. Stevens Company.

Of special interest to collectors are cap bombs, particularly those made as figures, such as the Yellow Kid (an early comic-strip character), the Admiral Dewey, the Uncle Sam, the Devil, and the two-faced Chinaman. A number of animated cap pistols were also manufactured during this period. Animated pistols have a figure or figures atop the barrel. When the trigger is pulled, the figures go through their antics, bumping, kicking, or hitting one another. The action culminates with the cap's being exploded. Most of these pistols were manufactured during the 1880s and 1890s and are somewhat rare today. Again, surprisingly, many of these animated pistols were made by the Ives Company and not by the big producers of mechanical banks, who were originally credited with their manufacture.

A Royal Pistol (1878). It is one of a group of desirable animated cap pistols. Upon firing the pistol, a cap is exploded and the top is released to fall to the floor and spin. As might be expected, the tops took quite a beating and were often broken. The pistol pictured has its battered, but original top still attached. C. L. COLLINS.

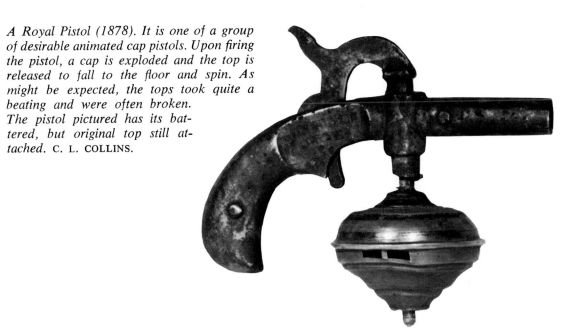

Be wary when buying animated cap pistols. Like most other cast-iron toys, they have been reproduced, and many of these facsimiles are very well done.

BELL TOYS

Regardless of the material used in their construction, bell toys constitute a group unto themselves. By definition, a *bell toy* is a toy that will ring a bell at certain intervals while being pulled or pushed across a floor. The most interesting examples have one or two animated figures who do the actual ringing.

The early bell toys usually consisted of a simple pair of wheels with a bell suspended between them. As the toy was rolled along the floor the bell would ring. Many of these toys had bells that were shaped like two cups pressed together. Inside was a marblelike piece of metal that would clang back and forth. Others had actual bells suspended on a post between the wheels, so that the bell would remain in place while the clappers would move back and forth to create the sound. Of the variations on these two simple designs, the most common had a tin horse connected to the wheels. As the toy was pulled along, the horse led the way.

While all bell toys are eagerly sought out, the most popular group has to be the animated ones, which, by the 1880s, dominated the scene and rivaled the actions of the mechanical banks of the same period.

East Hampton, Connecticut, the center of bell production in the United States from 1860 to 1900, produced an incredible array of bells for schools, homes, and businesses. The transition to the manufacture of toys that incorporated bells into their framework seems a natural one given this background. At hand were all of the component parts and, more importantly, the engineering genius necessary to create fine bell toys.

The Gong Bell Company of East Hampton was the giant of the bell-toy industry. According to an advertising brochure of the mid-1870s, the company started operations in about 1866. At that time it was producing bells for home and industry, including the "Abbes" Patent Gong Door and the Alarm Door Bells. Sleigh bells were also part of its inventory, as were simple rolling chime toys. By the 1880s, the Gong Bell Company had become the country's largest producer of bell toys. One can only marvel at the extensive line illustrated in one of its catalogs.

An Independence Bell toy (1876). Here is a great toy with everything going for it except a known manufacturer. Obviously manufactured for the centennial celebration of 1876, the toy has a patent date of 1875. The base consists of two cast-iron shields that rest on four heart-shaped wheels. This wheel design was used on some toys manufactured by the Gong Bell Company as well as the J. E. Stevens Company. The wheels are normally attributed to Stevens, which manufactured parts of toys for other companies as well as for itself. This is why some toys are mistakenly attributed to Stevens. There is a cast-iron eagle attached to the rear of the toy, and there may have been a flagpole stuck into the top of the bell at one time. Embossed is the name "Independence" and the dates 1776 and 1876. When the toy is pulled along the floor, a lever attached to the wheels rings the bell. This particular toy is not pictured in either the Waltross Company bell-toy catalog or the N. N. Hill Brass

Company catalog (both major producers of bell toys). Nor is this toy to be found in the catalog of the Gong Bell Company, probably the largest producer of bell toys. It was possibly manufactured by the Enterprise Manufacturing Company, which made numerous toys for the centennial celebration. RICHARD MERRILL.

The Waltrous Company, also of East Hampton, was established during the 1880s and apparently merged with the N. N. Hill Brass Company sometime before 1900. It is probably most noted for its simple rolling bell toys and its toys that were pushed or pulled by a stick connected to one end. Of a similar nature were the continued line of bell toys produced by the N. N. Hill Brass Company, another East Hampton–based firm, which was established in the late 1880s. Its two most sought after toys are the Jonah and the Whale bell toy and the comic-strip Happy Hooligan and His Automobile. (Happy Hooligan is especially desirable for its subject matter; and not only is it a comic-strip toy, but it is an automotive toy and a bell ringer too.) This innovative company was in business at least into the 1950s, producing bell toys of wood and tin.

One of the better-known manufacturers that carried a small but fine line of bell toys was the J. E. Stevens Company. Although better known for its mechanical banks and cap pistols, Stevens also produced the classic Baby Quieter bell toy. As the toy was pulled along the floor the action of a seated man rocked a baby on his knee and rang the bell. Stevens also produced the Swan Chariot, which was not actually a bell toy at all. As the toy was pulled along the swan's wings moved up and down while a small bellowslike affair caused the swan to honk. This toy was probably aimed to be popular among girls because of the combination of figures—a swan and a little girl. Another bell toy aimed at the same market was the Daisy Bell toy, manufactured by the Gong Bell Company. This toy had a girl and a doll as it principal figures.

Regardless of the nature of the toy or the manufacturer, bell toys are deemed worthy of note by most collectors because they transcend a number of collecting categories while still remaining a group all their own. And within this group, the toys that have special interest are those with political overtones and those fashioned after a popular comic strip of the period. Examples of bell toys with a political nature are the Uncle Sam and the Don, manufactured by Gong Bell during the Spanish-American War and later revamped as the Cossack and the Jap during the Russo-Japanese War, and the Teddy and the Rough Riders, manufactured by Waltrous. Among the comic-strips bell toys were the Buster Brown & Tige and the very desirable Captain and the Kids, both by Gong Bell.

No matter how old, new, simple, or complex they may be, bell toys have always fascinated children and collectors alike, and they continue to be one of the most highly sought-after and competitive groups of collectible toys.

GAMES

Old games, especially board games, have been gaining in interest and appeal with collectors over the past few years. For years these fine old games, with their beautifully lithographed boards and boxes, have been overlooked or spurned by collectors of "real" toys and have not had a fitting place in the toy world. Now, however, this situation seems to be changing. Old games are being searched out and preserved for their historic as well as aesthetic importance.

While there is some difference of opinion concerning when the first board games emerged in the United States, we do know that advertisements were appearing as early as 1819 for the Don Cossack, which was described as a new and interesting military game.

Although many of the games advertised at this early date were card games, some were also board games, a fact that presents a problem for collectors. The Mansion of Happiness, which was manufactured by the W. & S. B. Ives Company of Salem, Massachusetts, in 1843, was always thought to be the first board game introduced in the United States. This problem was noted in 1961, by Inez and Marshall McClintock in their book *Toys in America,* and it is still a matter of contention among different collecting factions and historians, despite the dated advertisements to the contrary. However, for our purposes a discrepancy of a few years is not of concern. What will concern us is why people collect games, how they go about it, what kinds of games are collected, and who the major publishers were.

Toy collecting as a hobby follows diverse avenues, but toys are toys regardless of whether they are made of cast iron or cardboard or whether they are two or three dimensional. Games are a form of amusement and, as such, are justly classified as toys. Card and board games were created to amuse young and old alike, and they were quite successful in the attempt. Games became a way of life during the early days of the nineteenth century and reflected our wars, inventions, attitudes, aspirations, and goals. While playing a game, the players are able to suspend themselves from reality and create a world of their own. Players become the many things that they had always wished they were, and through role playing they see themselves in a different light.

Quite often, games came packaged in beautifully lithographed cardboard or wooden boxes. And even if a game is incomplete, it is sometimes worth buying for the box alone. Many collectors use framed box covers as decorative and complementary pieces for display, an idea that becomes especially effective if the lithography relates to the collection. For example, collectors of model trains might include in their displays one of the following Parker Brother's games or puzzles dealing with the railroads: All Aboard for Chicago, The Railroad Game, or Railroad Picture Puzzle. All these were published on or before 1900 and are favorites among collectors. One should not, however, cut up a box for its cover if the game is intact. The box significantly increases the game's historic as well as monetary value.

Games are sometimes collected by type, series, or subject matter. Groupings that follow a central theme—such as cities, historical events, or travel by

A framed McLaughlin lithographed jigsaw puzzle (1888). C. L. COLLINS.

plane, train, or automobile—are of particular interest. A historical theme might include games about particular persons or events contemporary with the release of the game. A collection of games dealing with Teddy Roosevelt, Thomas Dewey, the Battle of Santiago, or the sinking of the Maine is an example of this type of theme.

Games such as the travelers Touring Series are also popular. Because the number of games that formed the series and the name of each game are known, a collector can acquire a complete set. In most other areas of toy collecting, this would be an almost impossible task. Imagine, for example, trying to locate an example of every tin automobile produced in this country!

Probably one of the best reasons for collecting old games is their relatively low cost. As the purposeful collecting of games becomes more and more popular and more organized, however, prices will undoubtedly rise. For now, one who perseveres can amass a nice collection of old games without spending a fortune.

During the 1860s, the "big six" in the field of game publishing were the W. & S.B. Ives Company and Parker Brothers, both of Salem, Massachusetts; the McLoughlin Brothers and Selchow & Righter, both of New York; Milton Bradley, of Springfield, Massachusetts; and Crandall, of New York and Pennsylvania.

The W.S.&B. Ives Publishing Company of Salem, Massachusetts (not to be confused with the Ives, Blakeslee Co. of Bridgeport, Connecticut) published a number of different games with varying degrees of success. The Mansion of Happiness and Dr. Busby were probably its two most popular attempts; Game of Pope as well as Master Rodbury and His Pupils were less successful. In addition to games and of a somewhat similar nature, the Ives Company also released at this time some very attractive *sand toys* (a boxlike affair with cutout cardboard figures enclosed within). Sand was poured into an opening

A Milton Bradley toy village (1910). Milton Bradley, a company most noted for its prodigious output of board games, also produced this toy village. Included were a street plan, figures, vehicles, and cardboard houses, which kept little builders occupied for hours. Because of its fragility, this is a difficult toy to find in complete and original condition. RICHARD MERRILL.

located in the rear of the box, and as it slid to the bottom, levers that caused the figures to move were activated. Sand toys are quite collectible, although not as popular as toys with some other mode of power.

Selchow & Righter published a few games but is probably best known for its "cut-up pictures" (puzzles). Most of its puzzles were lithographs of animals, birds, boats, and other common subjects that were pasted onto a cardboard backing and then dissected. One rare puzzle that attracts the eye of many collectors depicts a church, apparently an unusual subject for a puzzle.

Crandall, an important name in the field of wooden toys, also played an important role in the area of puzzles and games. In effect, many of its wooden toys had to be put together like a puzzle. In addition to this group, Crandall also manufactured some very fine blocks and some games that were played with blocks.

The two names, though, that stand out above all the others in the game field have to be Milton Bradley and Parker Brothers. Both of these companies have had illustrious careers spanning over the last one hundred years. By their prodigious output, they have made two Massachusetts cities, Salem and Springfield, the game capitals of the world. To list in these few pages even a small portion of the thousands of games published by these two companies since the 1860s would be impossible, but we would like to at least list a representative sampling of collectible board games, card games, and puzzles produced before 1930. Many toy collectors consider the years 1860 to 1930 to be the "Golden Age of Toys." During this period, Milton Bradley published:

Authors	Gold Hunter	Ring Board
Stars & Stripes	Canoe Race	Animals
Toy Shop	Donkey Race	Blockade
Old Maid	The Tourist	Writers
Smashed-Up Loco	The Race for the North Pole	Conette
Peter Coddle	The Yacht Race	Birds
Tin Peddler	Encounter	Combat
Toss Target	Conflagration	

Parker Brothers published:

All Aboard for Chicago	Automobile Puzzle
American History	Bicycle
Cut-Up Animals	Lotto
Cut-Up Loco	Havana
Hold the Fort	Street Car
Pat and His Pigs	Santa Claus
War of 1812	Rough Riders
Witchcraft	Jumping Turtles
Railroad Game	Little Cowboy

Last but not least are the McLoughlin Brothers, who published a number of colorful games and puzzles during the 1870s and 1880s, all of which are very collectible as well as difficult to find. Probably this company's best known games are Chiromagica (a fortune-telling game), Jackstraws, and Little Pets. What distinguishes the games by McLoughlin is that many came in wooden rather than cardboard boxes. Also, the lithography used was of the highest caliber. In fact, many artists are now collecting games by McLoughlin for their artwork alone. They are well worth the search.

MARBLES

Many a youngster can remember "knuckling down" to a game of marbles in the schoolyard and being either a happy winner or a saddened loser. All children play for keeps.

The collecting of marbles, for display rather than play, has been making great strides over the past few years, to the point where a professional organization, the Marble Collector's Society of America, has been established. This society is now in the process of donating a representative sampling of marbles to the Smithsonian Institute for permanent display.

The history of marbles can be traced back to the ancient world. The Egyptians, Greeks, and Romans all played games with marbles, usually made from clay or stone. Surprisingly, many of these marbles have survived over the years.

Marbles probably reached the height of their popularity in the United States during the period from 1850 to 1890. Apparently, though, until the later half of the nineteenth century, most of the marbles played with in this country were imported from Europe. It was during the late 1880s that American companies (that is, the Navarre Glass Marble Company and the National Onyx Company) started to manufacture marbles. Within a few years they were producing more than one million marbles per day, and by the 1940s they were producing more than four million marbles per day. Most of this production took place in West Virginia and Illinois, two of the largest marble-producing sections of the United States.

Early marbles were made from a number of different materials, including clay, stone, and glass. Many of the early glass varieties were hand blown and can be discerned by the *pointil marks*, which are small circular nubs left at both ends of the marble when it was broken away from the glassblower's pipe and the other marbles. Particularly rare is a marble with only one pointil mark, which indicates that this was the first marble to be cut free. More exotic marble materials were onyx, jade, cobalt, and marble. According to one source, marbles actually made from marble were called "taws" or "alleys." Taws that had dark red veins running through them were later called "blood alleys," a name that must have been popular with little boys!

Most marbles were manufactured in a uniform size of approximately one inch. Of course, there were those that were smaller and those that were larger. The really large marbles, those from three to five inches in diameter, are especially interesting because they were often used in an indoor game not unlike bowling. The larger ones were known as "carpet balls" and are especially popular with collectors. Unfortunately, they are difficult to find in good condition; usually they are quite chipped.

While most all early, hand-blown marbles are worth collecting, the most eagerly sought after are the *sulfides*, which are made of clear or, even more difficult to find, colored glass and have a figure of an animal or a face embedded in them. The rarer ones have two figures or a number encased in them or are busts of well-known persons contemporary with their manufacture, such as Jenny Lind.

Unfortunately, we must note here that sulfides have been reproduced by European glassmakers for the past twenty years or so. Luckily, they can be detected by a few telltale signs. Since the newer marbles were machine-made, there are no air bubbles surrounding the encased figure, as in the older ones. Also, the figures are usually one-sided, as opposed to the full-figured examples found in the older marbles. Finally, if there is no pointil mark, the marble is probably one of the later, machine-made ones, which, while still collectible, are not as valuable.

CONSTRUCTION SETS

Still another interesting but not especially popular group of toys consists of construction, magical, electrical, and chemical sets. In general, toys that are missing parts are usually shunned, and construction sets by their very nature fall into this catagory. Naturally, 100 percent complete construction sets are few and far between because there were so many component parts involved. And finding replacement parts, especially for electrical and chemical kits, is usually a difficult task. More often than not, as parts were used up they were discarded and not replaced. In addition, most of the earlier construction sets did not have each part marked with the manufacturer's name, and so a problem with identification arises. Many of these sets had parts that were similar in style, and this too creates an identification problem.

When discussing construction sets certain brand names always come to mind, and they are the ones that are most collected. The Meccano construction sets, manufactured in England, were one of the first to incorporate the idea of steel construction on a small scale. Started by Frank Hornby and although noted for its construction sets, the Meccano Company also manufactured other types of toys as well.

Struktiron sets, manufactured by the Ives Manufacturing Company for a short period of time between 1914 and 1918, came in both a motorized as well as a nonmotorized version. They ranged in price from $2 to $8. The sets that we have seen came in cardboard boxes with lithographed covers and included a well-illustrated catalog of projects. Like most Ives toys, the Strukti-ron construction set is a desirable addition to any collection, but even here, completeness is of primary importance.

Before 1916, erector sets were manufactured by the Mysto Manufacturing Company, which also produced a small line of toy trucks. About 1917, the owner of the company, A. C. Gilbert, decided to lend his name to the firm, thus changing it to the A. C. Gilbert Company. In addition to its well-known steel construction sets, the Gilbert Company also produced chemical and electrical sets, the Hudson Build-A-Loco train set, and a large truck-and-dirigible building set. Although erector sets are fairly common toys, the earlier ones came in wooden boxes and are very collectible. And while speculating on the future collectibility of construction sets is difficult, note that some collectors are now looking for early Lincoln Logs sets in good condition.

"NEW" TOYS

A number of recent articles seen in toy journals have been asking the question "Are Japanese toys collectible?" What they are really asking is whether the newer toys are collectible. By "newer," we mean toys that were manufactured after 1945. This question has challenged the tastes of the older toy collectors because it is a threat to their commonly held notion that the only toys worth collecting are those that were manufactured before 1930. As we have mentioned earlier, the "Golden Age of Toys" spanned the years 1860 to 1930, and many purists insist that toys from this period are the only ones worth mention.

The United States grew up as a nation during this "Golden Age," even though the process was not always pleasant. We suffered through the Civil War, a few minor foreign entanglements, and the war to end all wars, World War I. Ironically, World War I probably had a part in drawing this demarcation line of 1930 (although some collectors insist that 1920 is the cutting-off point). Until this time war was glorified, and every little boy wanted to grow up to be a soldier or a sailor. But this war changed American attitudes because it was not a "gentleman's war" like those in which we had previously fought. No conventional rules were followed, trenches were dug, a "no man's land" was declared, airplanes fought in the skies, and gas was used in the field. War became more mechanized, and modern warfare was born. And, without trying to sound too melancholy, a feeling of innocence was lost.

If you compare the toys manufactured before and after World War I, you can note a marked difference. Toys became a bit "harder" in nature after the war. The beginning of a detachment on the part of the manufacturer and an acceptance of an inferior product on the part of the consumer is especially evident in toys manufactured from World War II to the present. This is not to say, however, that toys manufactured after 1930 should not be collected; we are only saying that many collectors believe there is a definite difference in the style and the "feel" of earlier toys. The result of this difference was that the demarcation line was drawn. Whether there is an actual difference or not is a point of contention among collectors, and each has to make an individual decision.

The toys that are of concern to us at the moment are those that have been manufactured since the late 1940s. This group includes toys from many countries, including Japan. And even though these toys may not be every collector's cup of tea, there is enough interest in them to make the older, more established collectors sit up and take notice.

At numerous auctions over the past few years, the newer toys have been surfacing and usually outnumber the older toys by a sizable margin. The conclusion that we have drawn from this turnabout is that someone is buying them. Perhaps a whole new era in toy collecting is emerging with these newer toys' being purchased for various reasons, including their value as Americana as well as items for speculation.

There is no single contributing factor or reason to which to point for this shift in collecting habits, but rather a number of varying reasons, which, when taken as a whole, are quite valid. Older toys, especially those in good condition, are getting scarce. Good old toys surface now and again, but many of them have just disappeared from the market for now. When one speaks with collectors about inflation, many agree that good toys will not lose their value because they are tangible objects and have an accepted worldwide worth, like gold. Even though the value of money fluctuates every day on the market, the value of toys seems to be going in only one direction: up. How long this trend will last is anybody's guess, but for the present, toys appear to be a sound investment.

Older toys are also bringing unprecedentedly high prices at auction, a fact that tends to scare away newer collectors, and these prices have sparked a great deal of controversy as well as stronger competition. Higher prices are partly the result of inflation, but they also reflect a demand by numerous European collectors and dealers who have the exchange rate in their favor. There are many Europeans at auctions these days, since they can, in effect, buy for less, and they are doing just that. An interesting counterreaction is that American collectors and dealers are bidding pieces up to exorbitant levels in order to keep the toys in the United States, thus making profit very difficult for the European dealers to make on their purchases. Perhaps we are experiencing a wave of nationalism on the part of American dealers and collectors; but more than likely, they are keenly aware that, when all of the toys are in Europe, that is where they will probably stay. A wounded ego and the fear that toys will be placed out of their reach has spurred collectors and dealers into a new era of buying.

Also, newer toys are not especially difficult to find and may still be in their original boxes, adding to their value as collectibles. Many of them are at least fifteen to twenty-five years old, and they have an appeal for the emerging group of collectors under age thirty who either owned or longed for them as children and now find them within their grasp. The newer toys reflect the culture that the newer collector is more familiar with—the inventions and scientific breakthroughs of the last twenty years. Only naturally do they have an affinity toward them. And in addition, with the fear of reproduction hanging so oppressively over collectors, knowing that at least one group of toys is still free from forgery is comforting. One can buy newer toys with confidence and without having to be an expert.

CHAPTER 7

P*rotecting Your*
Investment

At a recent auction, thirty-four still banks and one mechanical bank were offered for sale. Of the group, only three were original—the others were reproductions. Only a few of the people there knew that the banks were not what they had been advertised to be. As a consequence, the final results were disastrous. People bid against one another for the "old" banks, and many of these banks sold for prices that only the originals should have realized.

Why didn't the auctioneer warn the bidders about the banks? Probably because he did not know that they were fakes. Why didn't we tell the others? The plain fact of the matter is that we did! Unfortunately, no one likes to be told that the article he or she wants to bid on, or is bidding on, is a fake. Most people like to consider themselves experts; and when a stranger points out a problem, they sometimes think that that person is downgrading the piece so that he or she can buy it without too much competition. Of course, we were interested in purchasing the three banks that were not fakes, and our bids did seem to prove that our advice was self-serving. For this reason, four very fine doorstops that had coin slots filed into them and eighteen newly created reproductions that had been aged were sold as old banks. (Aging a toy does wonders for its appearance, as we shall see later in this chapter.)

The moral of this story is simply that if you are not willing to do your homework, you only have yourself to blame for falling victim to an unscrupulous or unknowledgeable seller.

ASSESSING ORIGINALITY

Never before have collectors of antique toys had so much reference material at their fingertips. Numerous volumes dealing with specific areas of toy

A Joe Penner toy (ca. 1930s). Joe Penner was a comedian popular during the 1920s and 1930s. Manufactured by the Louis Marx Company, this tin lithographed toy is 8 inches tall and has Joe walking along and carrying a basketful of ducks (one of his standing jokes was the question, "Wanna buy a duck?"). As Joe shuffles along, his hat bounces up and down and his cigar wiggles. The same type of action was used by Marx in some of their Popeye characters as well as in the G-I Joe series. Since this is an earlier Marx toy and depicts a comic character, it is more desirable than some of the later toys by the same firm. RICHARD MERRILL.

collecting are available to the novice as well as the advanced collector, and each offers important data. In addition, reprints of early toy manufacturers' catalogs are available to the collecting public. Yet even these resources are not enough to tell the whole story. Because many early records were lost, and because pre-1900 toys were seldom marked by their manufacturers, we are left with a problem: How can we identify older toys as to manufacturer and originality? Some of our suggestions may seem obvious, but we have found through past experience that the obvious is quite often overlooked.

Try to determine the approximate age of a piece using its design, construction, and outward appearance as criteria. Is the toy hand-painted or lithographed? (Most hand-painted toys date to before 1920.) Is the toy made of tin, cast iron, pot metal, or a combination? (Review the characteristics of each group mentioned throughout this book.) How primitive is the toy? If it has wheels, are they fancy or plain? Is the paint original and how worn is it? Have other toys like this one come into your possession before? If you can determine the approximate age then you can discount numerous toy manufacturers. The type of toy is also a determining factor; not all manufacturers produced the same kinds of toys.

Determine similarities; they are not always enough to go on, but if a link can be made, some progress has also been made. Compare one toy to another. Are the castings the same or at least similar? How about the styling in general? Is the paint of a similar nature? These are factors to consider. Remember, however, that some toy companies made parts for other companies, and that some even sold toys from others under their own names. (At least they made it seem that way by advertising competitors' toys alongside their own in their catalogs, thus giving the impression that the toys were all manufactured by the same company.)

See and handle some good toys. Develop a "gut reaction" and test it.

A clockwork German paddle-wheeler, and a battleship moored atop its original box (ca. 1915–1920). The paddle-wheeler was manufactured by Oro-Werke of Brandenburg, Germany. The battleship, also from Germany, was manufactured by REB Company. Both ships are made of lithographed tin and were produced prior to 1922 when Oro-Werke went out of business. As is true of most box covers, the advertised product is a far cry from the toy's actual appearance. RICHARD MERRILL.

Decide which toys are worthwhile and then ask the person whom you deem an expert for his or her opinion. How often are you right?

Attend as many auctions and antique shows as possible. Keep a record of prices that are being paid; this will give you a measure of the value of your own toys. Talk with other collectors and dealers; see what they are buying and also what they are avoiding and why.

Research cannot be stressed too heavily. Whenever possible, use primary reference sources—old catalogs, advertisements, trade cards, documents, patent information—anything that you can get your hands on. Add to your library as many secondary reference sources as possible. Compare the information given in one with that given in another to find discrepancies, and then find out who was wrong. Old catalogs and advertisements are more valuable if they are in their original condition. Try not to cut up old magazines or catalogs in order to get the one or two ads that are needed. At least try to save the entire page that the ad is on. Another good idea is to file each ad into its proper category for easy reference.

Successful collectors are those who know their subject. You need not be a serious researcher to purchase a valued item from time to time, but to be consistent you must know, as often as possible, how to identify and assess what you have or might acquire. Identification is not an easy process, but it is a rewarding one.

FERRETING OUT THE FAKES

Collectors and dealers who have no expertise in the antique-toy field may fall victim to a well-constructed forgery. Of course, very few dealers knowingly risk their reputations by buying or selling fake toys. However, there are people in this field, as in most collecting fields, who will take a legitimate reproduction, age it, and then attempt to sell it as an original. The novice must be aware of this fact, since many of these reproductions are very good forgeries, and some are also older castings (twenty years or so) and are especially difficult to discern.

Most newer reproductions can be detected almost immediately by someone who has learned through trial and error to spot the difference.

Terminology

At this point, defining and discussing some common terms will be helpful.

Reproduction: A *reproduction*, or a "repro," is an article that is a duplicate of an original and is often made by using the original to create the mold. This practice is especially common with cast-iron toys. Pieces of the original

This toy, illustrated in an Ives toy catalog of 1893 as an Iron Hose Carriage with Running Horse and Driver, listed for $12.00 per dozen. From the flying mane of the running horse to the brightly colored paint on the hose reel, not much more can be said for an Ives toy other than "poetry in motion." RICHARD MERRILL.

are pressed into compacted, wet sand molds to create an impression. Molten metal is then poured into the impression. After the metal has cooled, the recast parts are painted and assembled, forming a new toy. Parts of a toy or whole cast-iron toys may be made in this manner. Collectors must be wary, then, of an original toy that may have a replaced part or two. The value changes dramatically if the toy has been altered in this manner.

Condition: Without a doubt, one of the key determining factors in the value of a toy is condition. The following five graduations of condition are the most accepted ones:

1. *Mint*: "Mint" should not be taken in the literal sense of the term, meaning the toy is brand-new and in the original box that has not been opened. In actual practice, the term is accepted to describe a toy in like-new condition, usually with the box. The toy has no scratches or chips and is 100 percent original.

2. *Near Mint*: Although not quite as fine as a mint toy, the near-mint toy does not have any major scratches or other damage. Again, it is 100 percent original.

3. *Excellent*: The piece is in nice shape, but it probably is chipped or shows signs of being played with. It has no missing or restored parts.

4. *Good*: The toy was really played with and has chips and scratches. There may be a minor piece missing, and perhaps there is some minor rusting.

5. *Fair to Poor*: The toy is banged up, and parts are missing or repainted. There may be some usable parts left, but the toy is very worn.

Repaint: Even if a toy does not actually work, if it is in 100 percent original condition, it will be worth far more than a toy that has been repaired or repainted. In the past, some collectors repainted their own toys to "restore" them and make them more visually attractive. This practice, fortunately, is not as common anymore. A repainted toy can be painted again to restore its original color. But it will still be considered a repainted or "restored" toy, and so its worth (both from a historical as well as a monetary standpoint) will be less than if it were in its original condition.

If a repainted toy is to be resold, the ethical thing to do is to mark the toy as such. Sometimes a good practice is to fasten a piece of masking tape with the word "restored" and the date to the underside of the toy, if this can be done without causing damage.

Some collectors who have purchased repainted toys have tried to remove the second coat of paint with paint remover. This is a painstakingly slow process, and it is not always possible to reach and preserve the original paint.

The accepted rule regarding the repainting of any old toy is "forget it." With every stroke of the brush some of the toy's value is lost. One exception to this rule is found in the field of train collecting. Although a repainted or "restored" train is not nearly as valuable as one in fine original condition, a train "restored" to its original condition is considered an acceptable collector's item.

Composite: A *composite toy* is one that has been constructed with parts from other toys. It is a fantasy toy and was never a production-line piece. Its value is in the parts used to create it rather than in the final product. A composite should not be confused with an original toy that has an original replacement part; such a toy is still considered to be original. In the area of composites, especially, a collector has to know toys. The parts are usually old, the paint is old, and the piece looks original; but did the toy ever come off an assembly line? If not, the only reason to buy the toy would be for its parts.

Old toy catalogs are especially valuable in determining authenticity. Most of the toys produced by any one company are listed, and so it becomes a matter of comparison. However, note that not all of the toys pictured were actually manufactured. A company sometimes decided, after its catalog became available, that a certain toy would not be successful and so it was not

An airplane and hangar (ca. 1920s). Logan Airport in Boston, Massachusetts, has grown a bit since this toy was manufactured. The wood and steel, single-engine plane has yet to leave the ground on its own power but, luckily, the hangar is always close at hand. The airplane and hangar were manufactured by the Andro-scoggin Paper Company (Toy and Novelty Division) of North Windham, Maine. RICHARD MERRILL.

produced. And just the opposite is also true: Many toys were produced that were never cataloged, especially old trains. After a while most collectors develop a "feel" for a toy. They just seem to know which ones to avoid or buy.

Variation: Most older toys were hand painted, and so determining whether a color is original or not is sometimes a problem. Standard colors were usually used, but there were many variations in design. For example, three color variations are found in some of the more common mechanical banks. The Speaking Dog bank was manufactured by two different companies, Sheppard and J. E. Stevens. The major difference is in the color of the dog. Stevens painted its dog a reddish brown, while Sheppard painted its a lighter tan color. Also, for some reason, the paint on the girl's face of the Sheppard bank tended to chip easily, and so this bank is usually in poorer condition than Stevens's version. The Indian Shooting Bear bank, also by Stevens, had a variation in the coloring of the bear. While most of the banks had a brown bear, a number of white bears have also turned up, even though they are a bit rarer. The Always Did 'Spise a Mule bank came with either a brown or a white mule. Apparently the brown version is the earlier one, but the white is rarer. Variations are also an important factor in train collecting. In addition to numerous variations found in the painted finishes, the variations in lithography are nearly endless. In fact, many train enthusiasts collect only the variations in lithographic design of one specific engine or car!

In addition to color or lithographic variations, there may also be differences in style and in materials used. If you find a fine old toy in a color, style,

A cast-iron sulky pull toy (ca. 1890). Pratt and Letchworth of Buffalo, New York, has always been associated with high-quality cast-iron toys, and the sulky pictured is no exception. Approximately 9 inches long, it is a classic example of the toy maker's art. The graceful but definite lines, the paint and casting quality, and the detailing of the horse combine to make this a classic example of a toy from the turn of the century. RICHARD MERRILL.

lithographic design, or material unfamiliar to you or not in accord with the accepted consensus about that toy, do not immediately dismiss the piece as a repaint or a reproduction. As long as the piece is an original, there is a chance that you may have discovered a rare variation.

Fake: A *fake* is a piece that is not what it is purported to be. In any field or collecting one can find fakes. The art world, for example, is full of faked masterpieces, and the toy world is no different.

In determining fake toys an important point to remember is that the price being asked should not be considered a factor. A fake is often displayed for an even higher price than the original would command. By setting a high price, the seller often misleads the buyer into accepting the authenticity of a piece before even examining it.

Composites are a form of fakery (whether intentional or not), as are reproduced, repaired, and repainted toys that have been aged and are not marked as such. Very few toy dealers sell such toys, and those who do are usually exposed. More often, one finds fake toys on the table of a dealer who also sells other types of antiques. Such a dealer may be an unwitting victim himself or herself and unaware that the toy is not an original. An old, original toy, especially a cast-iron one, will have hairline cracks in the paint. Check the paint under a magnifying glass; if the paint is not aged or grazed, it may be newer than you think. If a toy appears to be burned, it is probably a new toy that has been "aged" by burning the paint away. Paint ages gracefully unless abused.

GUIDELINES FOR THE BUYER

Examine the merchandise very carefully. Few toys, even the older ones, lose all of their original paint through normal aging processes and heavy play. The paint on some of the early, hand-painted toys has a tendency to flake easily. For example, Ives standard-gauge trains, which were not properly primed, are usually found with much of the original paint flaked or flaking. Even cast-iron toys do not usually lose all of their paint, though they do chip easily.

Beware of the toys that are a mass of rust or are covered with oily dirt. Other aging tricks are to submerge the toy in a salt-water bath for a few days, causing the paint to fade and rust to form, or to bury the toy in oily dirt or wet sand for a few weeks. Be able to spot the difference between old and new rust. New rust is usually reddish brown in color and much lighter than old rust. Remember that even authentic toys that are completely rusted are of little value to the collector.

When purchasing a cast-iron piece, always check the finish. If it is black, grainy looking, and rough to the touch, the toy could have replacement parts.

Check all suspect cast-iron toys, if possible, under a black light, which will enable you to discover any flaws or repairs.

Measure the base of a mechanical bank and compare it with the base tracings in *Toy Bank Reproductions and Fakes,* by Robert L. McCumber. Mr. McCumber traced the base plates of his original banks and compiled them into a working guidebook. Many reproductions are made using a mold cast from other iron banks rather than the original brass pattern. Because cast iron shrinks, a fake base plate will be noticeably smaller than the tracing of the original.

Always carry a magnet with you to test cast-iron toys. Check any section that you have reservations about, especially sections that appear to have been repainted. If the magnet does not adhere to a surface that you know it should adhere to, the section has been replaced or repaired. Remember another point about cast-iron toys: Each piece should fit snugly. If there are noticeable gaps, a piece may not be authentic.

Be careful when purchasing tin toys. Tin toys are more difficult and costly to reproduce than cast-iron toys, and so fewer reproductions are found. With tin, look for repainted sections, resoldered pieces, replaced parts, or holes indicating missing parts. Replacement parts for tin toys, especially the earlier ones (1870–1890), are scarce. Keep this in mind when contemplating the purchase of an incomplete tin toy.

Be aware of reproductions. Listing all of the cast-iron toys that have been reproduced would be impossible. However, banks are a little easier to account for as a result of McCumber's book and other literature on the subject.

It is known, for example, that the Book of Knowledge Encyclopedia Company reproduced a number of mechanical banks from its collection during the 1930s and 1940s. These repros are easy to spot because each has an embossed base stating what it is. In addition, there is a circular plastic insert also located in the base of each bank. While filing or grinding away the embossing would be possible, getting rid of the circular hole would be impossible. A number of these banks have recently turned up at auctions with the plastic insert popped out and the embossing ground away. When one of these banks is altered, not only might the buyer be deceived, but the value of the reproduction is lost. Of all the reproductions, those made by the Book of Knowledge are probably of the highest quality. They are being purchased by bank collectors and are sometimes substituted for a rare bank in a collection until the original example is found. A collection of these reproductions makes a nice display, but the banks are becoming difficult to locate. A few collectors, as well as a few toy companies (including some in Taiwan), have also made reproductions. While some of these are fairly accurate, most can be easily detected by a knowledgeable buyer. Even good reproductions are worth only a fraction of the value of an original.

When making a purchase, ask for a receipt and business card for your records. Ask the seller to note on the receipt that the toy is being sold as an original. This may protect you if the toy is not. If the seller refuses to grant this request, there may be reason to question the toy's authenticity and to decide not to purchase it. *Pass by any toy that is questionable.*

Although the following list of reproductions is incomplete, it should alert the novice to the fact that numerous reproductions do exist:

Mechanical-Bank Reproductions

Acrobats	Chief Big Moon	Magician
Always Did 'Spise a Mule	Clown on Globe	Milking Cow
(both types)	Creedmore	North Pole
Artillery Bank	Darktown Battery	Owl
Bad Accident	Dentist	Paddy and the Pig
Boy Scout Camp	Indian and Bear	Stump Speaker
Cabin Bank	Jolly Nigger	U.S. and Spain
Cat and Mouse Bank	Lion and Monkeys	

Still-Bank Reproductions

Andy Gump	Clown	Mammy with Spoon
Baseball Player	Cradle with Baby	Merry-Go-Round
Bear-Stealing Pig	Foxy Grandpa	Mulligan the Cop
Buffalo	Horse	Professor Pug Frog
Campbell Kids	Indian	Sharecropper
	Main Street Trolley	

DETERMINING VALUES

Whether buying or selling old toys, your own research is the best guide to their value and the best protection against paying too much or receiving too little. Remember the importance that condition plays in the value of a toy. The more complete a toy is, the more it is worth. A repainted or restored toy is worth only a fraction of one in its original condition.

Beware the buyer who downplays a toy that you know is a good example, and think twice about accepting an offer that you think is low. Beware the seller who overplays a toy that you are suspicious of, and rely on your own examination and knowledge to determine its fair value.

PRICE GUIDES AND CATALOGS

Price guides, listings (usually illustrated) of toys and their approximate retail values, are a continual source of amusement and amazement among toy collectors. This is not true in other fields of antique collecting, but in the toy world, with prices in an almost constant state of flux, price guides can tend to be somewhat troublesome. When working with price guides, you must be constantly aware of the fact that they tend to be obsolete before they reach publication. Up to six months may elapse between the time one is written and the time it is printed, and up to a year may have been taken to research, write, and compile one. So what we have is a finished product that has prices a year or so old listed. Over the past six or seven years, prices have tended to fluctuate so greatly that the figures given are, at best, ballpark figures.

Pricing systems, for the most part, are quite often arbitrary. They tend to reflect regional attitudes toward certain toys, and they quite often list the exception as the rule. For example, earlier we discussed two toys that were sold at auction this year, a common tin toy and a rare bank. Do not be surprised to see the inflated prices paid for these two exceptional cases being quoted in price guides this year and next. To get a true feel for values, you should visit antique shows and auctions, speak with toy dealers and collectors, and then decide upon the most accepted value.

To keep abreast of current values, many collectors and dealers subscribe to different auction-house catalogs. If a collector remembers that at any given

An ox cart, made by the Carpenter Company of Port Chester, New York (ca. 1890s), hauling a load of barrels past a wooden and paper lithographed stable, a product of the R. Bliss Company (1880s). RICHARD MERRILL.

auction almost anything can happen, the proper use of these catalogs can be helpful. They are a far better measure of a toy's actual worth than regular price guides are for a number of reasons. Unlike price guides, auction catalogs from reputable galleries often list condition and completeness of the toy as well as manufacturer, date of manufacture, and so on. Auction catalogs are more current in that they are constantly being printed. When you examine them over the course of a year or so, you can see how trends are forming and follow a particular toy's economic growth. Auction catalogs also indicate how a certain toy is valued throughout the country. For example, farm toys are not especially popular along the East Coast, but they are in heavy demand throughout the Midwest. If a collector has certain toys to sell, he or she can deduce where the demand is the greatest.

Our advice to the novice is to not look upon price guides as being the final word as to value but to judge their accuracy in light of his or her personal observations, experiences, and contacts with dealers and other collectors.

SPECULATION

When speculating about the possible future of toys manufactured after 1945, one important consideration is the manufacturer's name. For example, toys carrying the Buddy-L trademark are now being reintroduced. Since there is a demand for Buddy-L large steel trucks and trains of the 1920s and 1930s, does it naturally follow that their newer products will become collectors items in the future? One can only follow and identify trends. The trend today seems to be of a speculative nature. This being the case, there is every reason to believe that toys carrying a brand name will continue to be popular among collectors. Buddy-L, serving here as only an example, has been somewhat popular for a number of years, and recently the demand for its larger trucks and outdoor railroad has reached an all-time high. In fact, this demand for large automotive toys has even affected the Keystone line of heavy steel vehicles. For years, pieces by Keystone have been downplayed in preference to Buddy-L, but this situation seems to be changing.

Another important consideration is condition. If the toys are in fine original condition and have not been abused or restored, they are quite desirable. If, on the other hand, a toy has been tampered with, the owner may have a difficult time selling it. Condition is a primary selling factor.

Still another consideration is the number and type of toys that are being collected. Getting carried away and buying more toys than you know what to do with, is very easy, especially if the toys are small and inexpensive. If you become used to paying $50 to $100 per toy, as is often the case today, the temptation to purchase a toy for only $5 or $10 becomes great. And the more you spend, the easier spending becomes, especially if the seller will accept a credit card. What must be decided, then, is the number of toys you can afford to purchase and keep around for speculative reasons. Chances are that some time will pass before any real money can be made on them. In the meantime, your own collection may suffer as a result of having too much money tied up in these other toys. Most collectors face this situation at one time or another, and each must make an individual decision.

Times change, as do trends. Toys that are popular today may be ignored in the future and vice versa. With this fact in mind, one must search out toy types that seem to have some sustaining power. In our search we have found a few categories that seem to fit into this group: comic-strip toys, trains, banks, and mechanical toys.

Comic-Strip Toys

Any type of toy that uses a comic strip as its inspiration can be included here, games as well as comic-related paraphernalia. Within this group could be watches, toothbrushes, drinking glasses, comic books, movie projectors, and perhaps a thousand other subsidiary areas. Though not actually toys, in the true sense of the word, they are still complementary additions to any collection.

Earlier comic toys are especially popular, but many toys from the 1950s and 1960s are turning up at auctions and are being fought over by collectors. This group even includes toys made in Japan by such companies as Linemar. Often thought to be of inferior quality, Japanese toys are going to be one of the most popular collectible groups in the future. The comic-strip toys are only a small sampling that will help lead the way.

The Captain and the Kids, Popeye, Happy Hooligan, Buster Brown, Toonerville Trolley, and Felix the Cat were all popular comic strips in their day and, as such, were models for toys of all sorts. The comic strips of today are not too different, and the toys that are being manufactured to coincide with a popular character or strip will (or should) be popular with future collectors.

Superman, Batman and Robin, Spiderman, the Hulk, Pogo, and Snoopy are all staple characters of today's comic strips. They are extremely popular, and each has been turned into numerous toys. In twenty years' time, they will probably be as eagerly sought after.

The acceptance of comic strips in the United States has been something of a cultural phenomenon, and its only parallel is in our passion for television and the movies. Like the comics of old, heroes are created through the magic of film. And, carrying the passion to its logical conclusion, perpetuating the myth of the wide screen, toys related to specific movies and television shows are more popular than ever. Within twenty years Star Wars action figures will be as popular with collectors as trains are today. Society dictates this simple fact. These toys are part of our culture, as commercial as the idea may be, and they are an important link with what was and what will be. As society pro-

Two fire engines (1890–1910). The transition from horse-drawn to horseless vehicles is nicely shown in this comparative study of two fire engines manufactured by the Wilkins-Kingsbury Company of Keene, New Hampshire. With a few minor changes, a horse-drawn vehicle becomes a motorized one. The fire engine on top is a clockwork toy; the mechanism is located under the driver's feet. RICHARD MERRILL.

gresses toys will record this progression, and as each becomes obsolete another will take its place. To a collector fifty years from now, toys of today will be every bit as important as we now imagine the toys of fifty years ago to be.

Trains

Ever since their first appearance, trains have seemed to symbolize all that the United States has stood for. Without them, the United States would not be the nation that it is today. Trains opened this country up from one coast to the other, and they will always have a special spot in the heart of America's youth, or so it would seem. But what will become of trains one hundred years from now? Will they disappear and be forgotten as newer, more efficient forms of transportation are developed? Or will there be a revival of interest in them? No one can really tell, but one thing is for certain: Model trains are as popular as ever, and kids are buying them as quickly as they are being manufactured.

Over the past twenty years, trains have undergone some dramatic changes, the most obvious being in size. From standard (2⅛″) to O to 027 to S (⅞″) to HO to N and Z gauge, trains have grown progressively smaller, while the enthusiasm for them has grown by leaps and bounds. Today, the trains being collected are standard, No. 1, and O-gauge, for the most part. But tomorrow, HO may be the most popular collectible train. The smaller trains have many decided advantages over the larger ones, especially if the collector operates an active, working, layout. In the space that would be taken for one simple circle of standard-gauge track, one could run a dozen HO sets. Storage is another problem that can be solved with the smaller trains. In a relatively small space one can house an entire railroad.

So, give some thought to the smaller gauges. They may not seem like much, but in the future they may be the only trains reasonable enough to collect.

Space Toys and Robots

All indications point to space toys and robots as the group to get involved with, as far as speculation is concerned. Over the past four or five years, the market for space toys has grown from practically nonexistent to extremely active. One only has to look through an antique journal either here or abroad to see how popular this group is becoming. Even established collectors are advertising for space toys, and justly so. Again, they are a part of our culture and as such should be preserved. Perhaps they are not as aesthetically pleasing to the eye as an early tin toy, but that is, at best, a subjective observation. Fifty years from now collectors will be longing for the good old days when robots were in flower—and could be purchased for under $20!

Battery-Operated Toys

People are now collecting battery-operated toys. Again, the most popular ones are the early toys, but toys from the 1960s are also now being purchased. So, if you have a Charlie Weaver bartender toy or a Hippo Chief, perhaps you should consider purchasing more.

Plastic Toys

Why would anyone collect plastic toys? They are so easy to break and so cheaply made! Well, how many early plastic toys will be around twenty or thirty years from now? Although plastic seems to be a universally accepted material for the production of toys, imagining that many of them will survive is difficult. If the survival rate is low, the demand will probably be high. Buy a box full and store them away. No one will ever have to know until you are ready to reveal your hidden cache.

Epilogue

To end a book properly takes a masterful touch, but we are very lucky in the subject matter that we have chosen. No toy-collecting books really end. Instead, each one is just a start, a part of the puzzle that explains the fascination of young and old alike for a well-made toy.

The toy industry is a mystery in many ways, and why one toy sells while another fails is just one enigma. When people set out to collect old toys, they run into barriers everywhere, but that does not dampen their spirits. Toy collecting is a challenge and offers many rewarding hours of pleasure.

The hobby and the research necessary to be successful are very important. If one is a well-informed and satisfied collector, the hobby has proven to be of value.

This book, then, is just another beginning. We hope that it is of benefit to the novice and the advanced collector alike. It is not, and never was intended to be, an end in itself but rather a helpful beginning.

*Organizations*_____

The following organizations are open to toy collectors and offer much to novice as well as advanced collectors. Membership in more than one group can prove very beneficial.

Maerklin Enthusiasts of America
P.O. Box 189
Beverly, New Jersey 08010

Marble Collectors Society of America
P.O. Box 222
Trumbull, Connecticut 06611

Still Bank Collectors Club
62 South Hazelwood
Newark, Ohio 43055

Toy Train Operators Society (TTOS)
25 West Walnut Street
Suite 305
Pasadena, California 91103

Train Collectors Association (TCA)
P.O. Box 248
Strasburg, Pennsylvania 17579

A Toy Collector's Working Bibliography_____

Near the end of most nonfiction books the reader encounters the *bibliography*, the listing of books that the author has used during his or her research. These books have been singled out by the author to be of importance, and since the reader may wish to continue his or her own study of the subject area, they are listed. Sometimes the listing includes *annotations* (a line or two discussing the content of the books), but most often all that appears is the title, the author, and the publishing history of each book. While the listing is useful whether or not it is annotated, an annotated list is always to be preferred. To the serious researcher, it is vital because of the time that it saves. He or she does not have to pore through books that are of little value to get to the information needed.

In addition to annotating a bibliography, dividing one into categories is also helpful. Again, this saves the reader the bother of wasting time.

What we have done is to list not only the sources used during the research of this book but also numerous other sources that will be of use to the novice as well as the advanced collector. Many collectors will be surprised that there is such a wealth of existing material. As we have stated, there has never been so much material available to the public, yet no one seems to be aware of it. Many of the books available have been published by their own authors, and so publicity has been almost nonexistent. Other books, including those published by important publishing firms, have been offered on a very selective basis. The books have not been suppressed, but they have been aimed toward collectors and dealers alone. In addition, advertising has been held to a minimum and books have been offered through only a few sources, since the firms felt that the market was not sufficient to warrant an important advertising campaign.

Today there is an enormous amount of interest in old toys and collectibles in general. Books about toys are finding their way into bookstores and into the homes of the general public. While some collectors and dealers may argue the benefits and problems that will be encountered because of a better informed public, the change was inevitable. As soon as toys reached the status of "respectable antiques," the demand for reference materials was the next logical step.

"A good bibliography is worth its weight in gold!" Ask teachers, librarians, and researchers, and they will all attest to this fact. Most serious toy collectors agree that their libraries and reference sources are an extremely important part of their collections. Even the most knowledgeable collectors cannot keep all the answers in their heads, but at least they have someplace to turn to.

This bibliography is an important (perhaps even the most important) chapter in our book. Each entry is annotated, and each carries all of the publisher's information that we could find. Occasionally, we were not able to locate all of the information, but the relevant facts are given. In addition to books, we have included other sources, such as films, magazines, and catalogs. We have also set up categories to aid the collector. In all, this is more than just a list. There will be some noticeable gaps, areas that have been overlooked. Some older books have not been listed because we have tried to update our listing and make it as current as possible. Many books that were omitted have been out of publication for a number of years and are collectible items in themselves. In addition, there will be books published after ours has been written and before it reaches publication. Space has been left at the end of the bibliography for you to add them. This bibliography will continue to grow and collectors will become better informed, thus making this a true working bibliography.

TOY COLLECTING IN GENERAL

American Historical Catalog Collection. *Nineteenth Century Games & Sporting Goods.* Princeton, N.J.: Pyne Press, 1971.
>Uses the same sort of format as the FAO Schwarz book. Pages have been taken from the Peck & Snyder Catalog of 1886. Another fun book to go through for research and to compare prices.

Antique Toy World Magazine.
>Published monthly since the 1950s and probably the finest collector's magazine on the market. And one of the only ones. Includes feature articles written by acknowledged collectors on specific aspects of collecting. Many are illustrated. Also includes information about upcoming auctions, toy shows, and so on. An all around great magazine. Address is 3941 Belle Plaine, Chicago, Illinois 60618.

Boogaerts, Pierre. *Robot.* France: n.p., 1978.
>The first book to be written on space toys and robots. An interesting and well-illustrated book.

Botto, Ken. *Past Joys.* San Francisco: Chronicle Books, 1978.
>A great toy book done in a "toys as art" style. Pictures toys alongside full-size models, postcards, and so on, in a witty as well as humorous collage.

Culff, Robert. *The World of Toys.* London: Hamlyn Publishing Groups, 1969.
> A very concise history of toys from their earliest period. Well illustrated.

Daiken, Leslie. *Children's Toys Throughout the Ages.* New York: Spring Publications, 1963.
> A general, but important, history of the production of children's toys. Deals with ancient as well as modern toys. Many photographs and drawings.

The Encyclopedia of Collectibles. Alexandra, Va.: Time-Life Books, 1969.
> A most important series of books that discusses all aspects of collectible items, including toys helpe to capture some of the incredible spirit with which collectibles have come onto the scene. Contains articles well-written by experts in each field. Very useful in introducing the general public to this ever-widening field.

Foley, Dan. *Toys Through the Ages.* Philadelphia and New York: Chilton Book Co., 1962.
> An interesting history that mixes nostalgia with some folklore regarding toys. Covers the gamit of toy types with an ease of style not commonly found in books of this type. Well illustrated with photographs and drawings.

Fraser, Antonia. *A History of Toys.* London: Spring Books, 1966.
> Another history of toy development from ancient times, as the name implies. Devotes more space to dolls than to other catagories.

Freeman, Ruth and Larry. *Cavalcade of Toys.* Wakins Glen, N.Y.: Cenutry House, 1942.
> A difficult book to find because of the demand for it. One of the pioneer studies and still one of the best reference sources available. A very easy-to-read history of the development of the American toy industry to 1940. Well illustrated. A must book to own.

Harman, Kenny. *Comic Strip Toys.* Des Moines, Iowa: Wallace-Homestead Book Co., 1975.
> An important book for the comic-strip-toy collector. Shows an ease of style and a profound knowledge of the material that make it a pleasure to read. Traces the development of comic strips and subsequent toy representations from 1896 to 1960. Profusely illustrated.

Hertz, Louis. *Antique Collecting for Men.* New York: Hawthorn Books, 1969.
> Another book by the prolific Mr. Hertz, and despite the title, one that should be of interest to everyone. Discusses many aspects of antique collecting, including toys. An interesting look at Mr. Hertz's expertise in fields other than toy related.

———.*The Handbook of Old American Toys.* Weathersfield, Conn.: Mark Haber & Co., 1947.
> A small but excellent reference source. Mr. Hertz has always been

"the" undisputed pioneer in the realm of toy collecting. This is one of his earliest attempts at writing, and one can note the change in style that is evident when comparing this book with some of his later attempts. The more he writes, the better he gets. An important book to have in any collection.

————. *The Toy Collector*. New York: Funk & Wagnalls, 1969.

One of the most readable and enjoyable books ever. Not a reworking of his earlier *Handbook of Old American Toys*, but a completely new book. This is the book to buy in order to get "hooked" on toy collecting. Well illustrated and excellent. A must.

Kaye, Marvin. *A Toy Is Born*. New York: Stein & Day Publishers, 1973.

A general survey of toy collecting and manufacture.

Kimball, Ward. *Toys: Delights from the Past*. Lebanon, Penn.: Applied Arts Books, 1976.

A former cartoonist/producer for Walt Disney, Mr. Kimball has become a legend in his own time among fellow toy collectors. His collection is fabulous and his book is as comical as his personality. A fun book to read.

Long, Ernest and Ida. *Dictionary of Toys Sold in America*. 2 vols. Calif.: Privately printed,* 1971, 1978.

An incredible piece of research and one that should be in every toy collector's library. Together, the volumes list and grade over 2,600 toys that were sold in the United States from 1870 until the late 1940s. Each toy is illustrated, catagorized, described, and graded as to value and desirability. Important two volumes for dealers and collectors alike. A must.

King, Constance Eileen. *The Encyclopedia of Toys*. London: Crown Publishers, 1978.

Primarily a study of European toys. Was well researched and has an ease of style that makes it enjoyable to read. Set up in encyclopedic fashion and well illustrated.

McClintock, Marshall. *Toys in America*. Washington, D.C.: Public Affairs Press, 1961.

A well researched and quite desirable book. Traces the development of the American toy industry until the 1940s. Well illustrated and well worth owning. We believe this to be the first government-subsidized study of the field.

McClinton, Katharine Morrison. *Antiques of American Childhood*. New York: Bramhall House, 1970.

A fun book to read. Covers all aspects of toy collecting and history in

---

* Most privately printed books can be obtained on the market or through *Antique Toy World* magazine in Chicago.

an easy-to-read, delightful manner. Well illustrated. A nice general overview.

Munsey, Cecil. *Disneyana.* New York: Hawthorn Books, 1974.

Walt Disney toys and memorabilia have become quite collectible over the last six or seven years, and the trend is nowhere near finished. Covers the Disney collectibles made prior to 1965. A necessary source for the Disney collector.

Old Toys: The International Monthly Magazine.

A new international toy journal comes to the American market. A great magazine, though somewhat expensive—$27 per year. Includes many color plates, which make this magazine. Gives insight into the European market, its trends, and so on. Worth the investment. Address is Poststore bv, Postbox 305, Apeldoorn, Holland Ugchelsweg 99b

Perelman, Leon J. *Perelman Antique Toy Museum.* Des Moines, Iowa: Wallace-Homestead Book Co., 1972.

A marvelous book for the masochistic toy collector who enjoys drooling over photographs of someone else's collection. Contains fantastic photographs and accurate histories for each toy. The Perelman Antique Toy Museum is located at 270 South Street, Philadelphia, Pennsylvania. Featured are approximately 3,000 toys manufactured from 1860 to 1920. A great book and an even greater museum.

Pressland, David. *The Art of the Tin Toy.* New York: Crown Publishers, 1976.

One of the most fascinating and visually marvelous books about toys to reach print. Covers the "Golden Age of Toys," from 1850 to 1914, and throws in a few newer toys at the end. An essential book for the serious collector of tin toys, especially European tin toys. Geared toward the European toy especially. A large format book and a welcome addition to any library.

Schroeder, Joseph J., ed. *The Wonderful World of Toys, Games and Dolls: 1860–1930.* Chicago: Follett Publishing Co., 1971.

A collected sampling of catalog pages, advertising, and illustrations that displays the toys, games, and dolls from the period mentioned. A fun book to go through to compare original prices with what the toys are now commanding. A nice piece of research.

Schwartz, Marvin. *FAO Schwarz: Toys Through the Years.* New York: Doubleday & Co., 1975.

A compilation of catalog pages from over the past seventy years. Shows both the growth of the company as well as the changes in the style of toys in general. FAO Schwarz, located in Boston and New York (among other major cities), was one of the largest retailers of toys in the world for over seventy years. It opened for business during the early 1860s and became one of the important outlets for toy manufacturers. The company is, in fact, still in business today, but it reached its heights during the "Golden Age of Toys" (1850-1914).

Tops. Charles Eames Production, 1969.

A unique, nonnarrated film featuring a cast of over 120 spinning tops from all over the world. Eight minutes long; in color. May be rented from the Boston University Library.

Tubbs, D. B. *The Golden Age of Toys*. New York: Time-Life Books, 1967.

Another marvelous picture book with the same sort of format and color photographs as *The Art of the Tin Toy*, by Pressland. Again, has an overriding emphasis on the European toy (pre-1930), but still is a must to own. Fun to read and informative. A great book.

Weltens, Arno. *Mechanical Tin Toys in Color*. Dorest, England: Blandford Press, 1977.

A handy little source book of European toy manufacturers. Includes a short history of European toy production along with a listing of trade marks to help identify old toys. As the name implies, deals with tin toys that are clockwork, electric, or friction driven. Also includes some glimpses of toys seldom seen in the United States.

AUTOMOTIVE

Bossi, Marco. *Auto Hobby*. Torino, Italy: Privately printed (we believe), 1976.

An important book for the collector of European autos. Mr. Bossi has long been a leader in the collecting of European-made automobile toys, and his book reflects this leadership in its knowledge and depth. He is also the editor of a magazine by the same name.

Hertz, Louis. *The Complete Book of Model Raceways and Roadways*. New York: Crown Publishers, 1968.

A how-to-do-it book dealing with the building of model raceways and roadways to compliment and authenticate a toy-automobile collection. Includes a section on building scenery, peopling the setup, and setting in the cars and trucks to create an impressive diorama.

————. *The Complete Book of Building and Collecting Model Autos*. New York: Crown Publishers, 1970.

A companion piece to the previous book. Hertz is more concerned in this treatment with the building of model autos than with their display. Covers building, painting, and so on during the first half of his book. Deals with the collecting of manufactured and already-assembled toy autos in the second section. Traces the history of toy autos in an interesting and informative nature, as do all the books by Mr. Hertz. Another important book to own.

Williams, Guy. *The World of Model Cars*. Des Moines, Iowa: Wallace-Homestead Books Co., 1967.

> Covers the whole range of model cars—history, manufacture, and so on from tin plate to plastic. Well illustrated.

BANKS

Bellows, Ina Hayward. *Old Mechanical Banks*. Chicago: Lightner Publishing Corp., 1940.

> Apparently the first book ever written on the subject of mechanical banks, and surprisingly enough, written by a woman. A difficult book to locate owing to the fact that it is out of print, but copies do show up. And even though there are a number of mistakes within the text, it was an admirable attempt. Practically nothing was known about mechanical-bank manufacture prior to this book, and Ms. Bellows did a superb job of researching and logging what was available.

Freeman and Meyer. *Old Penny Banks: Mechanical and Still*. Watkins Glen, N.Y.: Century House, 1960.

> An important bit of research, which is still available. Two well-known experts in the field teamed up for this attempt. A necessary book for the bank collector.

Griffith, F. H. *Mechanical Banks*. New York: Privately printed, 1972.

> A paperback version of an earlier book, updated and improved by the acknowledged expert in the field. Contains a grading system set up by Mr. Griffith—not prices, just levels of rarity and desirability. Another important book.

———. "Old Mechanical Banks." *Hobbies—The Magazine for Collectors*.

> A fine magazine made even nicer by Griffith's articles. Has included, in each issue since 1954, a section on mechanical banks. Address is *Hobbies* magazine, 1006 S. Michigan Avenue, Chicago, Illinois.

Hertz, Louis. *Mechanical Banks*. New York: Privately printed, about 1950.

> A highly prized collector's item in itself. A valuable resource book printed in manuscript form. Unfortunately only about 200 copies were printed.

McCumber, Robert. *Toy Bank Reproductions and Fakes*. Glastonbury, Conn.: Privately printed, 1970.

> An essential reference book for the mechanical-bank collector. Consists mostly of base tracings of original mechanicals. Designed for the prospective buyer to measure the bank being considered against the tracings in the book to ascertain whether the bank is an original or a fake. Fakes and reproductions will measure slightly larger or smaller than the original tracings. Especially important for a novice collector to have.

Meyer, John. *A Handbook of Old Mechanical Penny Banks.* Lancaster, Penn.: Rudisill & Co., 1952.

    Meyer's first book and a classic in this catagory. Even though somewhat dated, still an avidly sought reference source. Includes price guide; amusing to note the rise in prices over the last twenty years.

Penny Banks. Al Davidson, 1974.

    A short movie that provides information about toy mechanical banks produced in the United States about the turn of the century. A fun movie to watch as the banks go through their antics. Ten minutes long; 16MM; in sound and color.

Rogers, Carole. *Penny Banks: A History and a Handbook.* New York: E. P. Dutton, 1971.

    A great book about banks. Most space devoted to mechanical banks, but stills also mentioned. Most photographed banks are from the Mosler collection and are probably the finest examples known to exist. A well-researched and easy to read history.

Whiting, Hubert B. *Old Iron Still Banks.* Manchester, Vermont: Privately printed, 1968.

    The still-bank collector's bible. Probably the only book available devoted entirely to old still banks. Includes fine photographs and charming captions, making it very desirable to own.

CAP PISTOLS AND EXPLODERS

Best, Charles W. *Cast-Iron Toy Pistols, 1870–1940: A Collector's Guide.* Englewood, Colo.: Privately printed, 1973.

    Offered in a limited edition, signed by the author. Really the only book of its kind in the field. A necessary book for the cap-pistol collector. Covers the development of the cap pistol from 1870 to 1940. Mr. Best is "the" expert; book is excellent in its scope and depth. Can be obtained from Rocky Mountain Arms and Antiques, 6288 South Pontiac, Englewood, Colorado 80110.

REPRINT CATALOGS

The following list is a small portion of the reprinted toy and bank catalogs that have been made available to collectors in recent years. Although these reprints do not have the charm or monetary value of the originals, they still do possess the relevant research material necessary for the collector. All of these catalogs are available through *Antique Toy World Magazine* (3941 Belle Plaine, Chicago, Illinois 60618).

    American Flyer (trains)—1926, 1930
    Arcade Toy Company—1926, 1932, 1933 (cast-iron toys)

Buddy-L Toy Company (large steel toys)—1925
Gong Bell Company (bell toys)—1902, 1903, 1905
Hubley Flyer Supplement—1930 (cast-iron toys)
Hubley Flyer Supplement—1933 (cast-iron toys)
Hubley Toy Company (cast-iron toys)—1920, 1932, 1934
Hull & Stafford American Toys (tin toys)—1870s
Ives Toy Company (toys and trains)—1906, 1923, 1928
Kenton Toy Company—1911 (cast-iron toys)
Kenton Toy Company (cast-iron toys)—1927
Kingsbury Toy Company—(cast-iron, steel, and tin clockwork toys)
Lehmann Toy Company (German tin toys)—1900s
Lionel Train—1911, 1920, 1922, 1931 (trains)
Marshall, Field (department store)—1892
Pratt & Letchworth (cast-iron toys)—1892
Schoenhut Toy Company (wooden toys)—1935
Tootsietoy (miniature autos)—1925
Tyron Toy Company—1927 (assorted tin and rubber toys)
Vindex Toy Company—1920 (iron toys and banks)
Wilkins Toy Company (cast-iron toys)—1911
A. C. Williams Toy Company—1911 (cast-iron toys)

MODEL SOLDIERS

Military Modeling Magazine.
> A London-based publication that deals with all aspects of collecting and displaying as well as creating and dressing toy soldiers. Published by Model & Allied Publishers.

Polaine, Reggie. *The War Toys.* New York: New Cavendish Books, 1979.
> The first history of the German firm of O&H Hausser, manufacturers of the Elastolin line of toy soldiers and accessories. A great book for the collectors of juvenile militaria.

PRICE GUIDES

Cranmer, Don. *Banks: Still Banks of Yesterday.* Gas City, Ind.: L-W Promotions, 1972.
> A fine collection of still banks pictured in black and white with the prices that they were commanding in 1972. Dated, but a nice reference source.

———. *Cast Iron and Tin Toys of Yesterday.* Gas City, Ind.: L-W Promotions, 1972.
> A handy reference source, but again, dated. A number of rare and unusual toys are found here.

———. *Cast Iron and Tin Toy Price Guide*. Gas City, Ind.: L-W Promotions, 1977.

> An updated version of Cranmer's earlier book, with a number of new additions. Interesting to compare price changes from 1972 to 1977.

———. *Collector's Encyclopedia of Toys and Banks*. Gas City, Ind.: L-W Promotions, 1977.

> New and bigger than ever. Over 900 toys illustrated. Cars, trucks, tin toys, cast-iron toys, horse-drawn toys, and still and mechanical banks all included, in addition to an updated price guide.

Greenberg, Bruce C. *Greenberg's Price Guide to Lionel Trains*. Sykesville, Md.: Greenberg Publishing Co., 1977.

> More than a price guide; actually a running narrative, in photographs, of the development of the Lionel train line from 1906 to 1942. Includes O-gauge, 027-gauge, and standard-gauge trains. Describes each train and train component, and then prices them according to condition. A very useful book for the train collector.

———. *Greenberg's Price Guide to Lionel Trains (1945–1977)*. Sykesville, Md.: Greenberg Publishing Co., 1977.

> Another important reference work for the collector. Picks up where the previous book leaves off and carries the topic through to 1970, when Lionel was purchased by Fundimensions, which has continued the Lionel name until the present.

OBrien, Richard. *Collecting Toys: An Identification and Value Guide*. New York: Crown Publishers, 1979.

> A very nice reference source. More than just a price guide; contains articles on toys as well as accurate photos and descriptions, which aid in identifying old toys. Current and useful.

RAILROADING

Alexander, Edwin. *The Collector's Book of the Locomotive*. New York: Clarkston N. Potter, 1966.

> A nice reference to railroadana. Includes railroad collectibles, such as lanterns, occupational mugs, stationery, literature, and so on, as well as trains. For the real railroad buff.

Fraley, Donald S. *Lionel Trains: Standard of the World*. Strasburg, Penn.: Train Collector's Association, 1976.

> A book published by the TCA and made available to the general public, although most of TCA's publications are for members alone. Covers the "Golden Age" of Lionel trains (1900–1943). Has over 700 color photographs with running commentary that traces the history of the Lionel line.

Godel, Howard. *Antique Toy Trains*. Hicksville, N.Y.: Exposition Press, 1976.

> A slim volume, but well done. Very well illustrated and easy to read. A book well worth owning.

Gomm, P. G. *Older Locomotives: 1900–1942*. London: Thomas Nelson, 1970.

> A fascinating little book that deals primarily with European trains, and some of the more obscure ones at that. Well illustrated and informative.

Hare, Burke and Wolken. *Toy Train Treasury*. 2 vols. Pittsburgh, Penn.: Iron Horse Productions, 1974.

> Narrates the history of the toy train in photographs and commentary. A nice set of books to own.

Hertz, Louis. *Advanced Model Railroading*. New York: Simmons & Boardman Co., 1953.

> As the name suggests, covers the third step in model railroading, the advanced stage. For the serious railroader interested in having a picture-perfect layout.

————. *Collecting Model Trains*. New York: Simmons & Boardman Co., 1956.

> One of Mr. Hertz's most popular and enjoyable books, and one that is much sought after, since it is out of print. A must for the serious researcher. Covers the history of the train industry in the United States and subsequent collecting interest over the years. Great.

————. *The Complete Book of Model Railroading*. New York: Simmons & Boardman Co., 1951.

> A general overview of the basic aspects of the hobby. Includes layouts, planning, gauges, building cars and locomotives, scenery tricks, operating, and so on.

————. *Making Your Model Railroad*. New York: Thomas Y. Crowell Co., 1954.

> A construction manual for the building of cars, locomotives, scenery, and so on. A complimentary book rather than a restatement of previous material.

————. *Messrs. Ives of Bridgeport*. Weathersfield, Conn.: Mark Haber & Co., 1950.

> One of the best by Mr. Hertz. A biography of Edward Ives and his son, Harry. A true story of the American ideal; a rags-to-riches story told in a thoroughly entertaining manner. An engrossing book and a necessary one for anyone interested in the Ives Toy Company.

————. *Miniature Railroad Service and Repair Manual*. New York: Thomas Y. Crowell Co., 1955.

Covers the service of old trains as well as the repair of broken models. Again, as is stated, using authentic (old) parts in making repairs is best.

————. *Model Railroad Conversion Manual*. New York: Thomas Y. Crowell Co., 1955.
For the railroader who wishes to run an old model train on house current. Includes all the steps necessary to complete the conversion. Covers the building of new motors, replacing parts, and so on. Today, among most toy and train collectors, the idea of converting or otherwise artifically altering an old toy or train is considered a bit sacrilegious. Also, if a conversion is made, the monetary value and historical significance of a piece is destroyed.

————. *New Roads to Adventure in Model Railroading*. New York: Simmons & Boardman Co., 1952.
Primarily an idea book for model railroaders. Complements *The Complete Book of Modeling Railroading,* and is a perfect book for intermediate-level model railroaders.

————. *Riding the Tin-Plate Rails*. Weathersfield, Conn.: Mark Haber & Co., 1944.
One of Mr. Hertz's early books, and one of his finest. Probably the pioneer study at the time. An absorbing study of the tin-plate train in America. An important research book and one that is, unfortunately, difficult to find.

Levy, Allen. *A Century of Model Trains*. New York: Crescent Books, 1974.
A train book that complements *The Art of the Tin Toy,* by Pressland. An outstanding book for photography and running commentary. Should be retitled *A Century of European Model Trains,* however, as its major emphasis is on the European examples.

Lionel Postwar Trains in Action. T. M. Productions, 1976. Write Train Collectors Association, Strasburg, Penn.
A film that shows what those trains on the shelf really did. Railroad sounds synchronized with the action of the trains, accessories and animated toy cars and people. Twelve minutes long; super 8MM; in color.

McComas, Thomas, and Tuohy, James. *Pre-War O-Gauge Lionel Trains*. Wilmette, Ill.: Productions, 1975.
An extensive but slim volume that depicts the variety of O-gauge Lionel trains, engines, cars, and equipment manufactured prior to World War II.

————. *Post-War Lionel Trains*. Wilmette, Ill.: T. M. Productions, 1976.
Picks up where the previous book left off. Covers trains manufactured into the 1960s.

Minns, J. E. *Model Railroad Engines*. London: Octopus Books, 1973.
A fascinating book. Includes photos of early European trains with commentary.

Model Railroading Unlimited. Kalmbach Publishing Co., Liberty Pictures, 1975.
A film that presents a brief demonstration of the history of model railroading and how easy it is to fall under the spell of an old train set. Twenty-five minutes long; 16MM; in sound and color. Write Train Collectors Association, Strasburg, Penn.

Sutton David. *Complete Book of Model Railroading*. Englewood Cliffs, N.J.: Prentice-Hall, 1964.
Covers most of the aspects of operating a model railroad, as well as some history of railroading as a hobby.

Train Collector's Association. *Dad's Trains and Grandad's Too: Trains from the Bill Krames Collection*. Strasburg, Penn.: Train Collector's Association, 1958.
A fascinating look at a fellow collector's train collection. The book that most train collectors would like to have written about their own collection but are apprehensive about doing because of theft and so on.

———. *Ives Trains: The Illustrated Catalog of Ives Trains and Trolleys, 1901–1932*. Strasburg, Penn.: Train Collector's Association, 1967.
The definitive study, so far. An absolutely necessary source for the collector of Ives trains. At the moment, another Ives book is being prepared by members of the TCA, which will be the most comprehensive attempt made to date.

———. *Picture Catalog of Lionel Standard-Gauge Trolleys; 1906–1915*. Strasburg, Penn: Train Collector's Association, 1967.
Another book in the TCA Collector's Series. For those interested enough to research into the development of the Lionel trolley. A good reference source, but hard to come by.

AIRCRAFT

Hertz, Louis. *The Complete Book of Model Aircraft, Spacecraft and Rockets*. New York: Crown Publishers, 1968.
A book about an area of collecting that has seen an upsurge of interest in the past two years and will be of considerable importance in the future. A good book to memorize.

Index

safe banks, 10, 60
sand toys, 102-103
Sears, 28
Selchow & Righter Company, 102, 103
selling, 40
semimechanical banks, 95
Sheppard Hardware Company, 34-35, 93, 116
Smithsonian Institution, 104
source materials, 29-35, 109-110, 112
  advertising materials as, 33-34, 112
  boxes as, 35, 112
  manufacturers' catalogs as, 29-33, 51, 111, 112
  patent information as, 112
  trade cards as, 34-35, 112
space toys, 11, 124
Speaking Dog bank, 94, 116
speculation, 121-124
  in battery-operated toys, 124
  in comic-strip toys, 122-123
  in plastic toys, 11, 124
  in robot toys, 124
  in space toys, 124
  in trains, 123-124
Stanley Manufacturing Company, 61
"Star Wars" toys, 122
steam accessories, 66
steamboats, 63
steam toys, 62-67
  dating of, 66-67
  dry ice in, 67
  firing of, 67
Stevens & Brown Company, 51, 91
still banks, 11, 18, 27, 28, 60, 93
  cast-iron, 92-93
  manufacturer identification of, 93
  reproductions of, 109, 119
  subjects of, 93
  value of, 93
Strauss & Company, 54, 89
Struktiron toys, 105-106
sulfide marbles, 105
  reproductions of, 105
"Sunday toys," 44
Surrey with a Fringe on Top, 61
Swan Chariot, 99

Tammany bank, 32, 94
terminology:

of fake toys, 112-117
of trains, 71-73
theft, 7, 35-37
tin banks, 91-92
tin toys, 7-8, 11, 46-54
  composites of, 52
  dating of, 51
  earliest, 46
  of 1850s-1860s, 46-51
  of 1860s-1890s, 51, 52
  examination of, 118
  jobbers in, 53
  manufacturer identification of, 51, 52-53
  missing parts of, 52, 118
  number of, 51, 54
  reproductions of, 52
  twentieth-century, 54
  value of, 53-54
Toy Bank Reproductions and Fakes (McCumber), 118
toy collecting:
  classifications in, 28-29
  as hobby, 5-7
  as investment, 7-11
  quantity vs. quality in, 25-28
  reasons for, 1-3, 125
  speculation in, 121-124
toy industry, roots of, 41-42
toys:
  attraction of, 3-5
  cleaning of, 39-40
  condition of, 113-114, 121
  as cultural mirrors, 5, 75, 100
  displaying of, 37-39
  "Golden Age" of, 103, 106
  modern warfare and, 106
  moralistic, 41, 42, 44
  new, 106-108
  restoration of, 39-40, 114, 117
  sources of, 12-24
  World War I and, 106-107
Toys in America (McClintock), 100
trade cards, 34-35, 112
Train Collector's Association (TCA), 35, 75
trains, 11, 27-28, 55, 67-87
  accessories of, 79-81
  books on, 31, 75
  cast-iron, 67, 69, 78